Alexander Rogers

Emendations in Aeschylus V. 22

With a few others in Sophocles and Euripides

Alexander Rogers

Emendations in Aeschylus V. 22
With a few others in Sophocles and Euripides

ISBN/EAN: 9783337280017

Printed in Europe, USA, Canada, Australia, Japan

Cover: Foto ©ninafisch / pixelio.de

More available books at **www.hansebooks.com**

THE
Blessings of Polygamy
DISPLAYED,

IN AN

AFFECTIONATE ADDRESS

TO THE

Rev. MARTIN MADAN,

Occasioned by his late Work, entitled

THELYPHTHORA,

OR,

A TREATISE ON FEMALE RUIN.

Give instruction to a wise man, and he will be yet wiser, Prov. ix. 9.

By RICHARD HILL, Esq.

LONDON:

Sold by J. MATHEWS, in the Strand; C. DILLY, in the Poultry; and by J. EDDOWES, in Shrewsbury.

MDCCLXXXI.

DEDICATION.

TO

All good WIVES in the Kingdom,

The following Pages

ARE HUMBLY DEDICATED

BY THEIR REAL FRIEND

THE AUTHOR.

THE

Blessings of Polygamy, &c.

Jan. 15, 1781.

Rev. and dear Sir,

HOWEVER exalted my ideas of friendship may be, (and I hope I do not exceed the language of humility, when I say that I trust what little I know of religion has rather *refined* than *diminished* them) however great and unalterable may be my regard for you, a regard founded on many years experience of the real worth of the person on whom it is placed; however highly I may respect you as a man of abilities and a scholar; above all, however much I may honor and reverence you as a minister of that gospel from which alone we both look for salvation; yet, where

where truth is concerned, I must forego every other consideration, and say with one of old,

Amicus Plato, Amicus Socrates, Magis Amica Veritas.

But why should I suppose I am acting contrary to friendship in thus publicly addressing you on the subject of your late work? With pleasure I call to mind the many happy seasons we have had together, when speaking of those delightful themes which will afford matter of joy and praise to the redeemed throughout eternity, how often I have been quickened and edified by your Christian conversation; how often comforted and directed by your judicious and seasonable advice; whilst on the other hand, you yourself have not disdained to hearken to the words, and have not despised the counsel of a friend, though so much below you in every gift both of nature and of grace. Let me not therefore harbor the thought that I can forfeit your esteem, because I tell you with all that sincerity and openness with which I have

always

always been ufed to accoft you, that I moft cordially wifh your book entitled THELYPHTHORA, had never feen the light; as I am now moft fully perfuaded of the fad truth of what I told you in a private letter, when I earneftly befought you to fupprefs it, viz. That the doctrine it advances is totally repugnant to fcripture, and is calculated to do irreparable mifchief in the church of God, and to the world in general. Thefe in few words are my undifguifed fentiments on your " TREATISE ON FEMALE RUIN;" and yet I am *as* fully perfuaded that your own intention in compiling and writing it was perfectly good, and that uprightnefs towards God, and benevolence towards multitudes of your poor miferable fellow creatures, at once dictated your words and guided your pen.

If any thing I may offer fhould prove the means of convincing you how exceedingly you have erred from the truth, your wonted friendfhip will caufe you to thank me; if you fhould ftill retain your opinion, the fame friendfhip will at leaft caufe you to conclude that I mean well. In either case therefore, I hope there is nothing wrong in my undertaking; though I confess I have been long struggling with myself, before I could resolve thus publicly to take the field of controversy against you: I trust however, that in this combat, I shall make use of no other sword than *that of the Spirit, which is the word of God* [A], and then though (to use a familiar phrase) I should *give you a home thrust,* yet I doubt not but we shall make up the difference without a second on either side, and agree together in this, *That faithful are the wounds of a friend* [B].

I am sensible it will afford a singular pleasure to many, that we have thus entered the lists together. But let *such* unhappy persons enjoy *such* pleasure. It is of no better sort than that which the malice of Satan excites, or rather it is that which excites Satan himself, when he can cause *Judah to vex Ephraim, or Ephraim Judah.* But it is a melancholy consideration that

[A] Eph. vi. 17. [B] Prov. xxvii. 6.

what will afford matter of malicious glee to the children of the wicked one, will prove the cause of heart-felt grief to the children of light.

Still truth is truth, and must not be given up, though Paul should withstand Peter, or though Paul and Barnabas should separate through the sharpness of the contention between them.—But I mention this by way of argument and allusion, not by way of comparison, at least so far as I myself am concerned.

I shall not attempt to follow you page by page, but at once *lay the ax to the root*, by striking at the foundation of what I look upon to be the leading principle or corner-stone on which you build the doctrine of Polygamy, viz. "That if God allowed a plurality of wives to his people under the Old Testament, he cannot have forbidden it to Christians under the New." This idea the erroneousness of which I shall endeavor to prove in various undeniable instances, has led you to offer the greatest violence to almoſt every text of ſcripture you have produced from the goſpels and epiſtles. Yet I bear you witneſs, that you have done this, not becauſe you were unwilling to admit the divine teſtimony, but upon ſuppoſition that you were making the ſcripture conſiſtent with itſelf, in order to prove the uniſon and harmony which ſubſiſt between the Old and New Teſtament.

We will readily admit that Chriſt came not to deſtroy the law; not to ſet up any new rule of conduct, any remedial law, or any more pure ſyſtem of morals than that which was before revealed by God in the ten commandments. So far from it, he came to *fulfill the law,* to *magnify* and *make it honorable,* to reſtore it to its original perfection, and to remove the falſe gloſſes which the ſcribes and phariſees had put upon it; to bring back the laws relative to marriage and divorce to their original and primitive inſtitution. Nor do I at all diſſent from you in believing that all thoſe parts of the ceremonial law, and of the Jewiſh polity which are of moral intendment,

ment, are and muſt be of eternal obligation; " unleſs God be pleaſed either to repeal theſe laws, or to give any other in their ſtead, as his infinite wiſdom ſees good." Obſerve, I lay an uncommon emphaſis on theſe words, and therefore I repeat them. " Unleſs God be pleaſed either to repeal theſe laws, or to give any other in their ſtead, as his infinite wiſdom ſees good." Which he certainly has a right to do, and frequently (as we ſhall ſoon make appear) *has* done, without the leaſt impeachment of his own moral character, or without the leaſt change in his own nature; foraſmuch as the one grand deſign which he ever has in view, and in which he is *without variableneſs or ſhadow of turning*, is his own glory, and the good of his church and people.

I would not from hence be underſtood to inſinuate that Polygamy was ever a part of the law of God. On the contrary, there is no command whatever which enjoins it, or even leans towards it, throughout the whole Bible. No, not in any caſe whatever.

ever. Not even when a man had no issue by a first wife, or though he were joined to a woman of the *haughty and refractory disposition of a Vashti* [C]. Yet to men unmarried God himself frequently condescends to give directions for the choice of a wife, as he did by an immediate answer to the prayer of Abraham's servant when he obtained Rebecca for Isaac. So throughout the whole book of Proverbs, there are various instructions for the choice of a wife,

[C] A very amiable and sensible lady one of the best of wives, and best of mothers, made the following remark to me on the note in the first vol. of Mr. Madan's Treatise, p. 182—" I do not perceive (said she) that queen Vashti did any thing unbecoming a good and an obedient wife, in not coming to the feast at king Ahasuerus's command; so far from it, that fear of exposing her husband seems to have been the motive of her refusal; for it is expressly said, that the king's heart was then *merry with wine*, and the very message itself shewed, that she was sent for that he and his guests *might look on her beauty*; so that the modesty of the queen might well be shocked on the occasion, and she had great reason to fear, lest had she at this time presented herself to this royal but intoxicated assembly, the consequences of her coming would have been much worse, than of her staying away."

with

with the highest commendations of a good one, and the dreadful lot and condition of the poor man who has the plague and torment of a bad one. Yet throughout the whole, God speaks in the singular number (*wife*) and never in the plural (*wives*). Nay there is one passage, which if we give the words their plain, easy scope, (and I shall not attempt to twist or darken them by any interpretation of my own) will nearly amount to a positive injunction of Monogamy [D], and consequently to a direct prohibition of Polygamy. The words are these, *Drink waters out of thine own cistern; and running waters out of thine own well. Let not* [E] *thy fountains be dispersed abroad, and rivers*

[D] For the benefit of the plain English reader I observe once for all, that Monogamy means the marrying or having only one wife at a time. Bigamy means having two wives at a time, and Polygamy (which Mr. Madan chiefly defends) having many wives at a time.

[E] Though I must confess myself to be no Hebræan, yet a friend of mine who has a critical knowledge of that language, assures me on the authority of the learned Mr. *Kennicot*, that this word (not) stands

in

rivers of waters in the streets. Let them be only thine own and not strangers with thee: Let thy fountain be blessed, and rejoice with the wife of thy youth. Let her be as the loving hind, and pleasant roe; let her breasts satisfy thee AT ALL TIMES, *and be thou ravished always with her love* [F].

But it is not my design in this place to produce texts of scripture against the doctrine of Polygamy. All I would insist upon is, that there never was any positive command of God which enjoined it, and that therefore it never was any part of the divine law. That he *permitted* it, either for the reasons that he permitted bills of divorcement to be given, or to prevent the

in some manuscripts; and indeed there is no making good sense of the passage without it; but on the contrary, it appears to be a contradiction of what goes before and what follows after, and the omission of it is exactly of the same kind, as you tell us the printer was guilty of, whom archbishop Laud fined so heavily in the star-chamber for leaving the same word [not] out of the seventh commandment.

[F] Prov. v. 15, 16, 17, 18, 19.

Jews,

Jews, who were a particular and diſtinct people, from intermarrying with idolatrous nations, is not to be controverted; and that he bleſſed the perſons and heard the prayers of his own people who practiſed it, and did not illegitimatize the offspring of thoſe polygamous marriages is alſo paſt diſpute. Still ſufferance is no law, even at the time it is granted; (elſe we make God the author of all ſin, ſince no ſin could have exiſted without his permiſſion) much leſs ought it to be extended and conſtrued as a law to after ages and people under different diſpenſations, and different circumſtances. I will not, however, reſt the iſſue on the diſtinction between a *permiſſion* and a *command*; I will even *ſuppoſe* (though I cannot *allow* what never appears to have been the caſe) that God under the Old Teſtament ordained certain laws in favor of Polygamy. Still he who ordained thoſe laws had an equal right to change or abrogate them as he thought fit and meet: and as his holy and ſovereign will is the only rule of right and wrong, I ſhall now prove by ſeveral undeniable inſtances that what

is

is agreeable to the mind of God at one time, and even matter of duty in his creatures to comply with, may at another time be absolutely wrong and sinful.

The *first* instance I bring shall be adduced from that almost original command of God. *Be fruitful and multiply* [G]. Now it is most certain that this command must have been fulfilled by the marriages of nearest relations at the time it was given, and for several years afterwards, as also immediately after Noah's flood; and this without any sin whatever in the persons so marrying; but when the world was peopled and the reason for such marriages no longer subsisted, then God forbad them both to Jews and Gentiles as unlawful, wicked, and incestuous. But if we were to adopt your grand argument in defence of Polygamy on this occasion, then we must say, that " God himself having instituted or permitted an incestuous intercourse among the immediate descendants of Adam and Eve and of the generations of Noah,

[G] Gen. i. 28.

under

under that great primæval command *increase and multiply*, and having blessed the persons and heard the prayers of those who practised it, and having adopted their issue as legitimate, therefore incestuous marriages can never be sinful under the gospel, and he who presumes to say that a brother may not now lawfully marry his own sister, attempts to be wiser than Jehovah himself, adopts the principles of Mahomet, Cerinthus, and Socinus, and in fact sets God and his Son Jesus Christ at variance with each other." How nearly this is your own language upon much more slender proof of what you have advanced, let those who have read your book judge.

The *second* instance I mention in proof of what I have said, shall be taken from the alteration of the sabbath. *For the seventh day God rested from all the work which he had made, and he blessed and sanctified it* [H].

[H] Gen. ii. 2.

In

In conformity with this early institution of the sabbath as a day of rest, the ancient people of God the Jews, observed and hallowed the seventh day with the most rigid severity, and you yourself bring some terrible examples of God's jealousy over this law of the sabbath, as contained in the fourth commandment, and of his indignation against the breakers of it; particularly in the fearful case of the man who was ordered to be stoned to death for gathering a few sticks on the sabbath day [I].—But he *who is the Lord of Sabbath*, has thought fit to change his own institution; and the day on which he rose from the dead, viz. the first day of the week, is now the great Christian sabbath, as the seventh day was that of the Jews. Whether the Jewish sabbath were or were not typical of the Christian sabbath, has nothing to do with the present question. The sabbath day is plainly changed. A poor man may now as lawfully gather his sticks on a Saturday as on any other day, and none but a Jew or a

[I] Numb. xv. 32, 33, &c.

Sabba-

Sabbatarian would deny him the priviledge. Nay even if he were to do it on a Sunday, especially for any necessary purpose, I cannot suppose that the rigor of the institution of the sabbath so far subsists, as that he would thereby incur the wrath of God, any more than by kindling a fire for preparing his necessary food on the sabbath day, which however was positively forbidden under the Mosaic dispensation.

In the *third* instance I bring I shall go farther, and shew that God under some particular circumstances absolutely commanded that to be done as an indispensible duty, which under others he has absolutely forbid as a most atrocious crime, and backed both his command and his prohibition by the severest penalties, and this was in the case of marrying a brother's wife after the death of the brother. Whosoever did this under the Levitical law, committed an act of sin and of uncleanness, and the curse of barrenness was pronounced against the woman with whom he was guilty, as it stands, *Lev.* xx. 21.

If

If a man shall take his brother's wife, it is an unclean thing: he hath uncovered his brother's nakedness, they shall be childless. But if the elder brother died without issue, then it became a duty absolutely incumbent on the next brother to marry the widow, and to raise up seed unto his brother, and the disobedience to this law was punished with death in the case of Onan [K].

The *fourth* instance I produce is from Ezra's exhortation to the people and to the priests to put away their strange wives [L], which no doubt he did by the direction, or at least by the full approbation of God himself, for the order was given immediately after he had addressed God in the most solemn manner by confession, humiliation, and prayer. Yet from the very first institution of marriage, those whom God had joined together, no man could put asunder. And when any man and a virgin had become one flesh (according to your own

[K] Gen. xxxviii. 8, 9, 10.
[L] Ezra. x. 1, 2, &c. throughout.

inter-

interpretation of the text, Deut. xxii. 28, 29.) *He could not put her away* ALL HIS DAYS, *seeing he had humbled her.* You will say, that this command of Ezra respected idolatrous wives and such only, and therefore these marriages were void *ab initio.* I will grant your assertion, but then you cannot abide by it yourself without throwing down the grand pillar which supports your doctrine of Polygamy; viz. that when *any man whatever* has become one flesh with any maid or virgin, this union is an absolute marriage in the sight of God: *He cannot put her away all his days, seeing he hath humbled her.* I say therefore, you must either raze one of the principal foundation stones on which you build the doctrine of Polygamy; or otherwise, you must allow the truth of what I am attempting to prove, viz. that under particular cases and circumstances, God frequently permits and allows that, which under different cases and circumstances he disallows and forbids, and *vice versâ*; still having nothing in view but his own glory and the good of his creatures;

so that he ever remains unimpeachable in his character of the God which changeth not, the same under the law, as under the gospel; the same *yesterday, to day, and for ever.*

Fifthly, Under the Jewish law bills of divorcement for other causes than adultery were permitted: by which the wife was dismissed from the house; and had liberty to marry another man; in which case, she could not return again to her first husband, Deut. xxiv. 1, 2, &c. [M]. But these divorces

[M] The words in our translation are just as follow, When a man hath taken a wife and married her, and it come to pass that she find no favor in his eyes, because he hath found some uncleanness in her: then let him write her a bill of divorcement, and give *it* in her hand, and send her out of his house.

And when she is departed out of his house, she may go and be another man's *wife*.

And *if* the latter husband hate her, and write her a bill of divorcement, and giveth *it* in her hand, and sendeth her out of his house; or if the latter husband die, which took her *to be* his wife;

vorces were pronounced abfolutely unlawful by Chrift himfelf under the gofpel; and whofoever put away his wife, and married another was deemed an adulterer; as was alfo the man who married her that was put away. This is clear from our Lord's own words to the pharifees when afking him of this matter. *Mofes becaufe of the hardnefs of your hearts fuffered you to put away your wives: but from the beginning it was not fo. And I fay unto you, whofoever fhall put away his wife, except it be for fornication, and fhall marry another, committeth adultery: and whofo marrieth her which is put away doth commit adultery* [N].

As I fhall have occafion in the fequel to confider this important fcripture more at large, I fhall only at prefent make fome animadverfions on a diftinction which you

Her former hufband which fent her away, may not take her again to be his wife, after that fhe is defiled: for that *is* abomination before the LORD, and thou fhalt not caufe the land to fin, which the LORD thy God giveth thee *for* an inheritance. ver. 1, 2, 3, 4.

[N] Matt. xix. 8, 9.

endeavor for obvious reasons to establish between the permission of Moses, and the permission of God himself in this matter of divorce. It is true indeed, our Lord says, "*Moses suffered you,*" but are we from thence to suppose, that God connived at what was sinful, because he either could not or would not thwart the will and pleasure of Moses? Is all scripture given by inspiration of God, or is it not? Did holy men of old speak as they were moved by the Holy Ghost, or did they not? Was Moses the vicegerent and legislator of God, or was he not? In a word, did he act by his own authority [O] or by that of Jehovah himself? I must certainly conclude that what was permitted or enjoined by the will of Moses, was permitted and enjoined by the will of God; and that to talk of Moses suffering a thing to be done which God did *not* suffer, is to set God and his own law-

---

[O] My friend has *almost* ventured to assert this, if not quite. His words are these "The only instance in which Moses acted by his *own* authority was in the matter of divorce."

giver

giver (or rather the executor of his own law) at absolute variance.—Our Lord says, *Did not Moses give you the law, and yet none of you keepeth the law?* Are we therefore to conclude, that Moses gave the whole law by his own authority? We have just as much reason to do so, as to suppose that he gave one jot or tittle of it by his own authority, whether we distinguish it by moral, ceremonial, or judicial. But what puts the matter beyond all dispute, is, that the whole of the divine law, in the very midst of which stands the passage in question, is ushered in with the greatest solemnity, as containing the mind and will of God himself, delivered to his servant Moses, who it is said, was *faithful in all things,* for the use of the people over whom he was appointed. And the conclusion of it is summed up in the following most striking words. *This day* THE LORD THY GOD HATH COMMANDED THEE *to do these statutes and judgments: thou shalt therefore keep and do them with all thine heart, and with all thy soul.*

It is therefore paft all doubt, that the law of God, and the law of Mofes, in every iota and punctilio, were one and the fame; and that Mofes in no cafe whatever fuffered any thing which the divine will did not authorife him to fuffer: Mofes could no more have permitted the cuftom of writing a bill of divorcement, than he could have fuffered the divorced woman, who had been defiled by another man, to return to her firft hufband, which he by the very fame authority which enjoined every other part of the law, ftrictly prohibits in the following words; *And if the latter hufband hate her, and write her a bill of divorcement, and giveth it in her hand, and fendeth her out of his houfe; or if the latter hufband die, which took her to be his wife. Her former hufband which fent her away, may not take her again to be his wife, after that fhe is defiled; for that is abomination before the Lord: and thou fhalt not caufe the land to fin, which the Lord thy God giveth thee for an inheritance,* Deut. xxiv. 4, 5.

I con-

I conclude all I have to offer on this head, by remarking, that when our Lord says, *Moses because of the hardness of your hearts suffered you to put away your wives,* it is just the same as if he had said, " Because of the hardness of your hearts this custom was suffered by the law of Moses;" but to suppose that Moses permitted it independent of God's authority, is to suppose that though God by his own infinite wisdom framed one part of the law himself, yet some inconveniences occurring relative to the laws of marriage, which he was not at first aware of, he left it to Moses to make the best of a bad bargain, and to get the people out of the scrape as well as he could.—Besides, if distinctions of this sort are once set up, in order to countenance any favorite opinion, we are not to wonder, if the words of Paul or Peter, or James or John, be thought of less consequence than the words of Christ; which would soon make way for the introduction of every abominable and pestilent heresy; as we know it already has done among many, who talk of the authority of the four gospels, in a

strain

strain as if they were to be regarded with higher veneration than the rest of the inspired writings.

Where it suits your own purpose, you find fault with bishop Patrick, for saying, " Moses himself supposes as much ;" which you observe, " looks as if Moses was speaking by his own wisdom ;" which the bishop did not at all mean to infer. But where it militates against your plan, and the bishop says, that " divorce (under the law) was allowed of God," there you " *take the liberty* to observe, that it is best to keep to the expression of scripture, and that our blessed Saviour does not say, that *God* allowed divorce, but *Moses allowed or permitted it.*" However in both cases, the bishop speaks on the supposition that what the legislator permitted, the Lawgiver had authorized, and that God and his law were in perfect union.

Before I quit this subject I shall only observe, that the divorced wives here, were not *idolatrous* wives, and yet they were suffered

suffered to be put away, and even to marry another man, living the first husband; which is a full answer to your objection concerning the command given by Ezra to the people to put away their *strange* wives. The same may be said of that passage, *Exod.* xxi. 10. *If he take him another wife; her food, her raiment, and her duty of marriage shall he not diminish.*—Moses is here speaking of the very particular case of a man who should sell his daughter to be a maid servant with a master who *humbled her,* or as it stands in the text, who *dealt deceitfully with her.*—And yet though he had been *one flesh with her,* God gave him liberty to put her away *if she pleased him not,* and to marry another.—Whatever this scripture may prove *for* you, it certainly proves this *against* you, viz. That the law, which declared that where *a man enticed a maid, and lay with her, he might not put her away all his days,* was not in all cases invariable; yet this is one of the principal texts on which you ground the doctrine of Polygamy, and argue in defence of it from the *invariable* nature of the law of God.

God.——But your grand miftake feems to lie in confounding the moral, with the judicial law, and in not perceiving that the latter, though blended with many excellent moral inftitutions, cannot poffibly fubfift, neither was intended to fubfift in any other nation than that peculiar one for whofe ufe it was framed. Such were the laws relative to theft, reftitution, damages, trefpaffes in cafes of truft, ufury, witchcraft, oppreffing of ftrangers, bribes, punifhment of fervants, &c. &c. &c. which are mentioned in the 22d and 23d chapters of Exodus, as well as in the book of Deuteronomy, and particularly the law of retaliation, which has fo much in it of moral intendment, that a late writer in a pamphlet intitled " A Letter to the New Parliament," feems almoft as anxious for its revival, as my friend Mr. Madan is for the revival of Polygamy, and *endeavors* to prove that our Saviour never meant to abolifh it. Yet there is no reafon to doubt from our Lord's own authority, *Matt.* v. 38, 39, that this law is now fuperfeded for that

more

more benign and evangelical fyftem which enjoins us to return good for evil.

Other inftances might be brought, but let thefe fuffice: and indeed I think if I had mentioned only one of them, that one would have been fufficient to eftablifh my pofition, that God confiftent with his own invariable nature and attributes, may, and does frequently permit, and even ordain that to be done, under fome cafes and circumftances, which under others he abfolutely forbids as wrong and finful. That therefore, notwithftanding he may have allowed and did allow Polygamy to have been practiced by his own people under the law, (though he never gave the leaft fhadow of a command for it), in order to preferve them as a peculiar people and diftinct nation, and to fulfil his royal promife, *that they fhould be as the ftars of heaven for multitude* [P]; yet thefe ends being

[P] It is a maxim founded on truth and on general experience, that the fame cuftoms in one country may have a quite different effect in another, according

ing now answered, God under the gospel, has been pleased to reduce the laws of marriage to their original institution, when he brought the first woman to the first man, and commanded that a man from thenceforth should leave his father and his mother, and should cleave unto his wife, and they twain should be one flesh; upon which

ing to the different laws, genius, and circumstances of the people, and according to the different ages of the world in which they live. Upon which account, though Polygamy may have been friendly to population among the Jews, and might without much inconvenience subsist with their political government, yet it would certainly have a very different effect in the present period among professors of Christianity, and even among the modern Jews, as well as be attended with a long chain of evils, of which the Israelites of our day seem fully sensible, by having given up the practice of Polygamy, and by contenting themselves with one wife. And indeed, when our Lord himself first made his appearance upon earth, a Polygamist was scarcely to be found amongst the Jews; which is a very sufficient reason, why in his public ministrations he gave no particular commands to his hearers *to put away all their wives except one*, when perhaps not one of those hearers who received his testimony, had any more wives than one to put away.

account

account Polygamy is so far from being allowed under the New Testament, that it ranks under the general name of adultery, as I shall endeavor to evince, by restoring several passages of holy writ to their plain easy natural sense, which I am heartily concerned to avow, have been dreadfully obscured and misinterpreted by the forced construction you have put upon them; but before I do this, I shall speak of the very dreadful and shocking consequences which must inevitably attend the establishment of your plan.

The Jews (as I before observed) being a distinct people, and separated by the nature of their laws and worship from all other nations under heaven, their great Lawgiver in his directions given to Moses, so suited their laws and government to their peculiar situation, and their situation to their laws and government, that these laws were enforced without any other difficulty than what the refractory disposition of that people sometimes occasioned, though in general they submitted themselves

selves peaceably to the decisions of Moses, and were unanimous in suffering those penalties and punishments to be inflicted on offenders which their laws enjoined; and when they were not so, God in a miraculous manner frequently interposed to the destruction of the disobedient. As they were under a particular institution by their judicial law in other respects, so they were in matters relative to marriage, divorce, seduction, whoredom, adultery, &c. not that the nature of these could at all alter, or that be sinful or not sinful in a Jew which was not the same in another person, but there were certain temporal punishments annexed to the breach of these laws, which did not subsist among other nations, and also certain miraculous methods of trying and detecting the guilty, which were only known among themselves.—Such was *the law of jealousy* [Q] to discover the unfaithfulness

---

[Q] *Numb.* v. 14. And if the spirit of jealousy come upon him, and he be jealous of his wife, and she be defiled; or if the spirit of jealousy come upon him, and he be jealous of his wife, and she be not defiled:

15 Then

faithfulness of a wife. And somewhat a-kin to it, (though not to be called miraculous)

15 Then shall the man bring his wife unto the priest, and he shall bring her offering for her, the tenth *part* of an ephah of barley-meal; he shall pour no oil upon it, nor put frankincense thereon, for it *is* an offering of jealousy, an offering of memorial, bringing iniquity to remembrance.

16 And the priest shall bring her near, and set her before the Lord.

17 And the priest shall take holy water in an earthen vessel, and of the dust that is in the floor of the tabernacle the priest shall take, and put *it* into the water.

18 And the priest shall set the woman before the Lord, and uncover the woman's head, and put the offering of memorial in her hands, which *is* the jealousy-offering: and the priest shall have in his hand the bitter water that causeth the curse.

19 And the priest shall charge her by an oath, and say unto the woman, If no man have lien with thee, and if thou hast not gone aside to uncleanness *with another* instead of thy husband, be thou free from this bitter water that causeth the curse:

20 But if thou hast gone aside *to another* instead of thy husband, and if thou be defiled, and some man hath lien with thee beside thine husband:

21 Then the priest shall charge the woman with an oath of cursing, and the priest shall say unto the woman,

culous) was *the cloth of virginity*, whereby to make known the reality of a maid [R].

woman, The Lord make thee a curse and an oath among thy people, when the Lord doth make thy thigh to rot, and thy belly to swell;

22 And this water that causeth the curse shall go into thy bowels, to make *thy* belly to swell, and thy thigh to rot: And the woman shall say, Amen, Amen.

23 And the priest shall write these curses in a book, and he shall blot *them* out with the bitter water.

24 And he shall cause the woman to drink the bitter water that causeth the curse; and the water that causeth the curse shall enter into her, *and become* bitter.

25 Then the priest shall take the jealousy-offering out of the woman's hand, and shall wave the offering before the Lord, and offer it upon the altar.

26 And the priest shall take an handful of the offering, *even* the memorial thereof, and burn *it* upon the altar, and afterward shall cause the woman to drink the water.

27 And when he hath made her to drink the water, then it shall come to pass *that* if she be defiled, and have done trespass against her husband; that the water that causeth the curse shall enter into her *and become* bitter, and her belly shall swell, and her thigh shall

maid [R]. But as these laws now no longer subsist, and evidently ended with the whole external Jewish policy, How would it be possible to adopt your system among Christians in the present day, so far only as the knowledge of virginity is concerned.—Suppose any artful woman who had a mind to marry some rich or great man, were to complain to any magistrate, or in any court of law, that he had *enticed her* and *humbled her*, and therefore she had a claim upon him to make her his wife; suppose

shall rot: and the woman shall be a curse among her people.

28 And if the woman be not defiled, but be clean; then she shall be free, and shall conceive seed.

29 This *is* the law of jealousies, when a wife goeth aside to *another* instead of her husband and is defiled :

30 Or when the spirit of jealousy cometh upon him, and he be jealous over his wife, and shall set the woman before the Lord, and the priest shall execute upon her all this law.

31 Then shall the man be guiltless from iniquity, and this woman shall bear her iniquity.

[R] See this also expressed at large, Deut. xxii. ver. 13 to 22.

twenty more were to do the same; how could the poor man help himself upon your plan? He must marry them all, and provide for them all, *seeing he hath humbled them, he may not put them away all his days.*

Again, let it be supposed, that any lascivious man who was tired of his first wife, hankered after variety, and wished to take another, or two, or three, or four, (for your doctrine allows of no limitation) he has nothing to do but to walk about a *wife-seeking,* make his proposals wherever lust and inconstancy shall suggest, and if the woman consent, neither he nor she commit any sin; *she has given herself up to the man of her choice,* who has *humbled her,* and therefore they are man and wife in the sight of God, without any marriage ceremony whatever.—But *he may not put her away all his days,* and he must *provide* for her——But suppose he is poor and cannot provide for her [S]; still *he may not put her*

[S] I am acquainted with a worthy good man, who in the honesty and integrity of his heart, having been

her away, so he and his wives must starve together, though most women in such a predicament it is to be presumed, would sally forth into the streets and supply their wants by prostitution, especially as nothing could be expected at home but quarrels, jealousies, and brawlings among the rest of the females, and at best, dissatisfied looks from a nauseated husband: So that if our streets abound with prostitutes and our stews with harlots at present, were your system to be universally adopted, London for its filthiness would soon surpass even Corinth itself, where Polygamy was practised without restraint, and where we have your own authority to assert that in the temple of Venus alone there were 1000, if not 2000 common whores.

Even among the Jews themselves who were curbed by such severe laws, what difficulties attended the practice of Poly-

been led away by the specious reasonings of *Thelyph-thora*, seriously meditated a design of abridging the book *to give away among the poor.*

gamy in the most regular and religious families! Witness the tyrannical authority of Sarah over Hagar, in the family of Abraham.—The disputes between Rachel and Leah in the family of Jacob; and the vexatious and taunting behavior of Penninah towards Hannah, in the family of Elkanah.

Is the case a whit better among the Mahometans, where Polygamy is established by law [T], than it was among the Jews.

To

[T] Your observation that the prohibition of Polygamy hinders the Turks from embracing Christianity, only proves, That the religion of Jesus Christ is far too pure and spiritual for the vitiated palate of a Mussulman; but it is no better argument for the toleration of Polygamy, than it would be for the toleration of drunkenness or covetousness, because if these sins could be dispensed with, many a miser or bottle companion might be made converts to Christianity. You also bring a quotation from Lord Kaim's History of Man, Vol. II. p. 89, where it is asserted, " That among the most zealous Christians in the kingdom of Congo, Polygamy is in use as formerly, when they were pagans; and sooner than give it up, they would renounce Christianity." But if the fact be true (which I much doubt) I cannot help thinking

To sooth the jealousy of the debauched Mussulman, and to prevent the apparent mischiefs which would be the effect of a plurality of wives under his own roof, the poor defenceless beings are generally locked and barred up in separate apartments, and none permitted to approach them but their antiquated *Duenna*, who being past all fears of exciting the passion of love in others, is suffered to go abroad herself.—But if Polygamy were ever to have the sanction of law in this land (which God forbid) the wives of Christians must either be imprisoned like many among the Turks, or else they must be suffered to dwell together under the same roof in their husband's house; in either case, what evils must follow! What tyranny in the husband is seen in the former, in the latter what jealousies and quarrellings among the wives, insomuch that all domestic peace must be bid adieu to. But above all, how is the case of the first wife to be pitied, especially if

ing that these *most zealous Christians* never had any Christianity to renounce.

she be of a meek, amiable, and affectionate disposition, when she is eye witness to the fact of others being received to her beloved husband's bed, and finds his love towards her to grow cool in proportion as it becomes warm towards a stranger? We often see the dire effects of jealousy on the most distant suspicion of unfaithfulness; but when that suspicion is exchanged for certain knowledge, what may we expect, or rather what may we *not* expect as the consequence!

But are matters likely to be at all more peaceable among a numerous brood of children by different wives than among the wives themselves? What disputes and wranglings about property, what dissentions among nearest relations must inevitably take place! insomuch, that one half of the men that are born must be brought up lawyers, to squabble about the *meum* and *tuum* of the other half; a large addition must be made to the courts of judicature in Westminster-hall, and county assizes at the *nisi prius* bar must last great part of the year.

It

It may be said, did not God know and foresee all this? Certainly he did know and foresee it, and therefore has most wisely forbidden the practice of Polygamy under the New Testament dispensation. Among the Jews these inconveniencies were not likely, at least not so likely to happen, circumscribed as they were by their own peculiar laws, and in every dispute about right and inheritance, subject to the immediate decision of Moses, or those appointed by him.

Again, Were Polygamy to be established by law in this kingdom, so far from encouraging honorable population, it would necessarily put the greatest check to it; since very few women of a modest, gentle, and affectionate spirit, and such only are fit for wives, would ever dare to embark in wedlock, lest the husband should take another wife, or as many more as he pleased, and thereby the first and only true wife, be deprived of that share in her husband's love, and that mutual union of heart with him which alone can make her life happy, and

and without which in proportion as her own love for him was great, her misery must be great also. And can that being deserve the name of a man, much less of a husband, much less still of a Christian, who could bear to see the amiable wife of his bosom in such a situation? Yet you must allow that this case might be a very common one, if Polygamy were tollerated by law. It is true, some bold, boxing Amazonians might be found who would not be afraid to venture themselves with any man, but then this would be upon the idea that *vi et armis* they should be able to turn all after-comers out of the house, and by force, if not by argument, speedily cure the husband of his love of Polygamy, and at the same time administer to him some wholesome discipline well enough suited to the nature of his crime.

Again, Suppose the legislature were really to take up the subject of your book, and to pass an act in favor of Polygamy; what would be the language of all the virtuous wives in the kingdom; " I'm sure,
" if

"if my husband thinks of taking another wife, I shall heartily wish I had never married." "Ah says another (who is unmarried) I think the men will not find it an easy matter to get good wives now a days; every honest woman will be afraid of having her nose put out of joint, by the introduction of a second lady into the family, therefore for my part I am determined to live single."—Hence an immediate decrease of honorable population [U].

But

[U] I had not put the above to paper more than a few days, before what I had conceived in theory, was confirmed by practice.—I have just had a letter from a friend, wherein he tells me that the match between a certain young gentleman, and a certain very amiable young lady, had been intirely broken off on her side, on information she had received, that the gentleman who was proposed to her was an approver of *Thelyphthora*.——Now suppose this young gentleman were to propose to several others, and were for the same reason to receive the same answer from all. What must he do? no woman will have him, for fear he should think himself at liberty to give his affections and his person to another. Hence he becomes

But let us suppose the act just now passed. The very next week how would our daily prints abound with paragraphs of treaties of marriage that were on foot being broken off, unless the husband would enter into articles not to marry any more wives whilst the first was living.—Hence again a sudden check to marriage, and thereby to honorable population.

Honorable population every where slackening its pace, seduction with all her dreadful train of deceit, abortive potions, and child murder will necessarily come in with gigantic strides, especially as it will be put in practice even by married men, with so much greater ease in proportion as the unhappy female is deluded under the specious notion of marriage. This idea comes tempted to commit whoredom, seduction, adultery, and what not. I do not indeed suppose that this will be the case with the young gentleman in question, of whom I entertain a very high opinion; but human nature is human nature still, and when checked in an honorable way, will seek gratification in one that is dishonorable.

will so far operate on those women who are in a lower station of life towards their superiors, that an uncorrupted maid servant will be a *rara avis* indeed; but the more *like a black swan* the more likely to escape [X]. Besides, what coquetting and flirting will be carried on in every assembly! what nightly walkings out! what *tendresses* and *douceurs* will there be between married men and young unmarried women! And are there not enough of these abominations practised already, that you, my dear friend must endeavor to wipe off the little shame which yet attends them; and in a manner authorize them before the world under the sanction of your respectable pen? Who will thank you for this service? Will virtuous wives? Will constant husbands? Will any parents who have the good of their children at heart? None I believe will think themselves indebted to you, unless it be the reverend editor of the Morning Herald for the many pretty, I might rather say, *smutty* paragraphs, which

[X] *Rara avis in terris nigroque simillima cygno.*

the

the legal adoption of your syftem would furnifh him with; or perhaps fome rich antiquated maids and old widows with large jointures, who will now no longer ftick on hand, as their fortunes will be very convenient to fupport the younger wives who have none.

Lewdnefs and feduction with their concomitant miferies are now in fome degree confined within a certain circle, which is diftinguifhed by the too gentle appellation of *the gallant world*; but bleffed be God, even in this degenerate day, there are very many families to be found where harmony and mutual love prevail; yet your fcheme (however undefignedly), actually tends to introduce all the evils of corruption and difcontent among thofe, who remain yet uncontaminated by the vicious cuftoms of this wanton and luxurious age; infomuch that every habitation where peace at prefent dwells, is liable to be turned into a temple of difcord, if not into an human flaughter houfe, by wives cutting their own, each others, or their hufband's throats, or hanging

ing or drowning themselves in fits of frantic jealousy.———Methinks, I am sitting quietly in my parlour in London, and am suddenly rouzed by the prodigious vociferation of two grim females of the right St. Giles's stamp, one on each side the street, and each of them holding one hand to her ear, crying, "Here is a full and true
" account of two most horrid, barbarous,
" bloody, and inhuman murders, which
" were committed on Friday night last,
" upon the bodies of Sir John Fickle, Bart.
" and his new wife, to whom he had been
" married only one week; which sad deed
" was done by his first wife, who after-
" wards stabbed herself with the same knife
" with which she murdered her own hus-
" band and his other lady, whilst they
" were asleep in bed together. Also the
" true copy of a letter to her own mother,
" which her ladyship left upon her table
" the night before she committed the
" murders, giving her own reasons for
" what she was about to do."

We may suppose the letter to run in the following words:

My dearest mother,

"YOU will shudder indeed when I tell you, that before to-morrow morning neither I myself, my husband nor his other wife will have a being in this world.—But my resolution is now unalterably fixed. You are my witness, God is my witness, that I have made Sir John a loving, faithful, and obedient wife for the space of six years. But his late marriage with Miss *Ogleman*, renders me distracted. O jealousy! who can live with thee in their bosom?—I cannot—I am desperate—Execration on the man who first brought Polygamy into this nation! Dearest mother, take care of my three sweet children which I have had by Sir John, to you the poor innocent babes look up for help. My hand shakes so much that I can hardly say, farewell—farewell.

"From your affectionate daughter,

"CONSTANTIA FICKLE."

Friday Night, 12 *o'Clock.*

I appeal to common sense, I appeal more particularly to those who have the finest and most delicate sensations; I appeal to those who know themselves, and who are experimentally and religiously acquainted with the workings of human nature, whether there be any thing throughout this tragical story, which wears the face of improbability, when Polygamy should be established by law.

In some part of your book indeed, after having enlarged on the blessings of Polygamy, your eyes seem opened to see the awful train of mischiefs which must unavoidably attend its introduction; and you would almost confine it to the single instance of a man with a woman who has been debauched by him. Where that man is *unmarried* he is certainly in conscience bound to make the woman his wife; and in every instance of this sort which comes before me as a magistrate, I always lay this down as matter of duty before the reputed father of a child: but when the answer returned is, " Please your Worship, " I have

"I have reason to believe that I am not the first man who has been concerned with her;" then, what can I say? for if that be a truth, and he marries the woman, he is not only linked for life to another man's whore, but according to your own system, to another man's wife, and so lives and dies in adultery.

But suppose the man be already a married man, then certainly his crime becomes much more heinous in the sight of God (though the purport of your book is to make him guilty of no crime at all, provided he persists in what he has done, and takes the woman to live with him), and by the Mosaic law he was to be stoned to death as an adulterer: however, you will not allow this to have been the fact, unless the woman were also a married woman; and in that case, you lament that the punishment of death is not now inflicted by our laws. That pecuniary fines for damages, are not in this case, a punishment adequate to the offence, I readily allow; but if the dread of the eternal vengeance

of

of God (which was typified by temporal punishments under the judicial law) will not deter men from these crimes I know not what will.—From the conduct of our Lord with the pharisees, when they brought to him the woman taken in adultery, it appears clear to me, that under the gospel, he *indirectly* at least, prohibited that either party in such case should suffer death, either by stoning or otherwise, as they were to do by the severity of the Jewish law; and as that man did by the extreme rigor of the same law, who was found gathering sticks on the sabbath day.

But I find I am deviating from my subject; in the discussion of which I was remarking, that in some parts of your book, you yourself seem so far sensible of the mischiefs which must necessarily attend your scheme, that you only defend it in some rare instances. Then, why in the name of God did you write *Thelyphthora*? Why cause all the dissentions you have caused in the religious world? Why give such cause of joy and triumph to those who

who treat every thing serious with contempt? Why grieve your friends? Why strengthen the hands of your enemies?—In any view let me repeat the question of my private letter to you—*cui bono scribere?*

Again, Were your plan to be universally adopted, I am persuaded, that so far from diminishing the legion of harlots that now swarm among us, it would greatly add to their number; and that almost every private house where the husband was a Polygamist, would be little better than a stew or brothel among the wives, who would certainly plead the inconstancy of the man they had married, in excuse for their own; for-as-much as he had first violated the conjugal tie, and disobeyed the apostle's command, by with-holding those duties which equally and reciprocally bind the parties to each other, and to themselves alone, in the plainest terms which words can express. " To avoid fornica-
" tion, let every man have his own wife,
" and every woman her own husband. Let
" the husband render unto the wife due
" benevo-

" benevolence, likewise the wife unto the
" husband. The wife hath not power of
" her own body, but the husband: and
" likewise also the husband hath not power
" of his own body, but the wife [Y].
" Defraud

[Y] I am under the necessity of observing, that whenever my learned friend finds an argument to be more than a match for him, he attempts to treat it with more than ordinary contempt. This draws off the attention of the reader to the assertion of the author, and thereby he is apt to overlook all the force of the reasoning which is presented to his view. Among these arguments which Mr. Madan thinks ought to be treated with this sovereign contempt, is that drawn from the words of St. Paul, " That a man ought not to have a plurality of wives, because the apostle all along restrains the number to ONE ONLY." His words are these. " To say that this text forbids Po-
" lygamy, because the word wife is in the singular
" number is mere trifling, as much so, as contend-
" ing that a man is to love but one neighbour, be-
" cause it is said, thou shalt love thy neighbour as
" thyself, not *neighbours*; or that he shall keep but
" one servant, because it is said, who art thou that
" judgest another man's servant." But supposing this argument more just than it is; still is not Mr. Madan aware that it is one of that sort which prove too much, as it may with equal justice be urged why

"Defraud ye not *one the other*, except it be *by confent* for a time, that ye may give yourfelves to fafting and prayer, and come together again, that Satan tempt you not for your incontinency." In all thefe texts there is juft the fame liberty given to the wife to be falfe to the hufband's bed, as to the hufband to be falfe to that of his wife. Should he therefore prefume to take to himfelf any other woman (except in fuch cafes where the law admits of divorce) might not the injured wife moft juftly and moft fcripturally complain, and fay, "My hufband to whom I have furrendered my hand, my heart, and my perfon, no longer treats me agreeable to thofe fo-lemn vows by which at the time of marriage, he pledged himfelf to me, and I to him. That benevolence which the fcripture enjoins from him to me I feldom partake of; he claims an exclu-

---

a wife fhould have more hufbands than one, as well as why a hufband fhould have more wives than one. But indeed it cannot be urged in either cafe, for there is fuch a reciprocal appropriation in the text, as binds the man to the woman alone, and the woman to the man alone.

"five

"five power over me, but in direct oppo-
"sition to the apostolic declaration, he
"denies that I have the same power over
"him, and therefore he defrauds me of the
"rights of the marriage bed, by bestow-
"ing his affection on other women, whilst
"I am left to burn with jealousy, or pine
"with disappointed love."

I can indeed conceive it possible for a woman to have so nice a sense of delicacy, that she would not choose to make a complaint of this sort even to her most intimate female friend; but then she is the more to be pitied on that account, as there is certainly nothing contained in it, which any woman of the most refined sentiments might not make even to God himself. However, though there might be here and there, such a meek, passive female to be found, yet I should judge, without censuring the sex, that they are not very numerous, but that multitudes under the above-mentioned treatment, could neither maintain their chastity, nor with-hold their rage; so that revenge and prostitution,

tion, seem to be the natural twin children of every polygamous intercourse.

It is but a short while ago, that a poor destitute woman applied to me for a letter of recommendation to be admitted a patient in the Lock Hospital, and urged in excuse for the bad disease she had contracted, that her husband had for some time past cohabited with another woman. It immediately occurred to me that this man was a true polygamist, or rather a bigamist, without the superstitious intermeddling of a priest. And that my friend, with his dedication to the governors of the Lock, Magdalen, and Misericordia, ought also to have preferred a petition moving that against Polygamy should be established by law, they would enlarge their wards and engage an additional number of surgeons.

But it is an affront to the clear language of the apostle in the texts cited from the seventh chapter of his first Epistle to the Corinthians, to attempt any explanation of them,

them, every word carries with it perspicuity and conviction, insomuch that one might think it were as easy to establish the doctrine of transmigration as of Polygamy from any part of the chapter; nay, much more easy, for it says nothing against transmigration, but says every thing which can be said against Polygamy: how then you could imagine that these texts or any of them speak only of a prevailing custom among the Corinthians of lending out their wives is to me inconceivable. Surely to use your own language, this is to make scripture speak any thing or nothing, or every thing, just as suits our own fancy. But neither will this forced interpretation stand, for in order to adopt it, you are obliged to change the word πορνειας which is very properly translated *fornication*, (or fornications) and to render it adultery, saying that it includes all sort of uncleanness. But why must the word πορνειας which comes directly from πορνη a harlot, be construed adultery rather than fornication? the reason is plain, because simple fornication could not be committed by the custom of lending

lending out wives, so you must either give up your sense of the text, or we must grant you that πορνειας in this place means adultery, and cannot mean fornication.— But I have still one objection to make against your interpretation; which is, that it intirely destroys the force of the apostle's reasoning in urging marriage as a remedy against the danger of celibacy. Of this you are aware, and therefore you will not allow this to be the drift of his argument. However, let us look back to the beginning of the chapter.

" Now concerning the things whereof ye
" wrote unto me; it is good for a man not
" to touch a woman. Nevertheless to avoid
" fornication, (δια τας πορνειας) on account of
" fornications, let every man have his own
" wife, and every woman her own husband."
It is most clear that St. Paul from the 1st to the 10th verse, is addressing himself to unmarried people, and to widows, advising continency as best suited to that distressed state of the church, if they were able to bear it; else he exhorts them to marry, and

and in case they should, he adds some directions for their conduct when married; after which he sums up the whole of what he had said in the following words: " I say,
" therefore, [which word *therefore* has cer-
" tainly a reference to what goes before] I
" say, therefore, to the unmarried and wi-
" dows, it is good for them if they abide
" even as I, but if they cannot contain let
" them marry, for it is better to marry
" than to burn."

In the tenth verse and not before, he turns his discourse to the married, and addresses them only. " And unto the married
" I command, yet not I but the Lord. Let
" not the wife depart from her husband,
" &c. &c."

All this is as plain as simple language can make it. How then you could possibly apply those words, *Let every man have his own wife, and every woman her own husband*, as a prohibition to those who had neither wives nor husbands to lend out, is to me most astonishing; but I cannot help saying

saying it is such a palpable perversion of sense and scripture as I hardly ever before met with. Yet even if this far fetched interpretation were to be allowed, it is as much a command to the wife not to lend out her husband, as to the husband not to lend out his wife: therefore take it which way you will it is big with absurdity.

But let us hear what you have to offer in defence of your opinion. I will transcribe your own words. " Those who re-
" present the apostle as addressing himself
" to single persons, and advising them to
" marry to avoid fornication, make him
" guilty of evident tautology—for the
" eighth verse is expressly addressed to the
" unmarried and widows, &c. &c. vol. I.
" p. 233." So it is, as also every verse before it: therefore here is no tautology, for the apostle is speaking all along to the unmarried.

Again, you add, " The very terms (of
" the second verse) shew it to be addressed
" to married persons; for how could the
" apostle

"apoftle fay to a fingle man—let him
"have ἐχέτω, retain γυναικα ἑαυτȣ, his wife;
"or to a fingle woman—let her have, i. e.
"keep to—τον ιδιον ανδρα, her own hufband?
"The immediate connection of this verfe
"with the three following, which can be-
"long to *married people only*, is another
"ftrong argument for the truth of this
"obfervation."——But I cannot allow it
to be any argument at all; and I appeal to
every one who has the ufe of their eyes and
reafon, whether every one of thofe verfes
which you fay belong to *married people only*,
do not belong to *unmarried people only*.
—For firft the verb ἐχέτω will bear no fuch
fenfe as you have put upon it—" Let her
"retain or keep to,"—and yet if it would
bear it, you have actually introduced it in
favor of Monogamy inftead of Polygamy;
for it ftands in the original as a direction
to the man as well as to the woman, and
therefore, if you will tranflate one part of
the verfe, " Let the wife *keep to* her huf-
"band," you are under the neceffity of
tranflating the other part, " Let the huf-
"band *keep to* his wife," for the Greek
word

word (εχέτω) is the same in both parts, therefore by endeavoring to make it speak what you wish in the one place, you have made it speak what you do not wish in the other place. How you will get out of this difficulty I know not, unless you can follow the example of your old friend Whittington, Lord-mayor of London, with his six bells, and persuade yourself and readers that by the *sound* of this same word εχέτω you are sure it means something very different, when addressed to a male than it does when addressed to a female, which will be literally *ringing changes.*—But as I observed above, the expression will not admit of the construction you have put upon.—*Let her retain or keep to*—but the plain signification of the word is *let her have*, or *let him have*: and would any man in the world, who knew what sense or grammar meant, say to a married man, Let him have a wife? or to a married woman let her have an husband? but the verb being in the imperative mood is plainly a command to *have* that which they have not already.

Secondly,

Secondly, If a tender parent were going to marry a son or a daughter, would he not give them directions whilst they were yet single, for their conduct after marriage, such as "Love your wife," "Behave well to your husband." In like manner St. Paul exhorting the unmarried who have not the gift of continency, to the use of the conjugal bed in order to avoid fornication, adds, "let every man have his own wife, let "every woman have her own husband. Let "the husband render unto the wife due be- "nevolence, likewise the wife unto the hus- "band. The husband has not power of his "own body but the wife. The wife has not "power of her own body but the husband. "Defraud ye not one the other, except it be "by consent for a time, that ye may give "yourselves unto fasting and prayer, and "come together again that Satan tempt you "not for your incontinency." Here is sense and reasoning in the apostle's language, if we suppose him to be addressing himself to the unmarried; but what sense or reasoning can be discovered, or where is the remedy he proposes against fornication, if we consider

consider him as speaking to those who are married already, in a way of exhortation not to lend out or interchange their wives? Give me leave to remind my learned friend who did not use to be averse to a little pleasantry, that whilst he is condemning our laws for the power they have committed to the priests of confirming marriages, he himself is claiming the authority of marrying half the church of Corinth; for I am sure that all those to whom St. Paul addresses himself from the first to the tenth verse, were ever esteemed unmarried persons, till that same good friend of mine coupled them together by his late interpretation of those texts.

I must now observe, that your labored criticism upon the words τον ιδιον ανδρα—*her own proper husband*, allowing it its full scope, has the same misfortune attending it as your construction of the word εχετω viz. it makes more against Polygamy than in favor of it, by not proving what you would have it prove, and by proving what you would not have it prove; for it implies

plies such a peculiar right and property which the woman has in that one man, as no other woman has or can have, insomuch that he is emphatically called *her own husband,* or *her own man;* which is certainly a much greater proof of the unlawfulness of his taking any other woman, than if the word had been in the feminine gender, and had been applied to the wife. I am therefore happy on this occasion to take your own words, and heartily agree with you, "that as all scripture is given "by inspiration of God, and the Holy "Ghost speaketh nothing in vain, there "is a weighty reason in giving the epithet "ιδιῳ to the husband;" that no man might ever suppose he had any power over his own body, so as to think himself at liberty to give the use of it to any other woman, but to her alone, who is so exclusively stiled by the apostle HER OWN PROPER HUSBAND.

After all, it cannot be denied that you have sent your lady *Polygamia* abroad in *a vesture of wrought gold,* but still I cannot think

think she is *like the king's daughter all glorious within,* for remove the ornamented mantle which you have thrown over her, and her deformity appears to view.

The idea of protecting the weaker sex, and of saving multitudes of them from ruin, is what gives a bias in favor of your plan; as you have dressed it up, to the humane and serious reader. But the mischievous and horrible consequences which must inevitably attend the practice of it, you intirely keep out of sight, though it is plain enough that they frequently stared you in the face; and this makes you attempt to draw the line between what you call *the wild licentious Polygamy of the Mahometans,* and a *holy and sober use of it.* But in the first place, I am astonished that a man who is acquainted with the depths and depravity of human nature, which is the same in England as in Turkey, should imagine any such line can possibly be drawn, if Polygamy were established by law.—Secondly, the grand argument which you yourself bring in defence of Polygamy, my, in a manner counteracts and prevents any such *holy sober* use of it: for the case in which you principally aim to establish it is between a married man and a virgin or maid that is *enticed* by him. Now such a man from the very act he has been guilty of, not merely in lying with the woman, (for this you will not allow to be any sin at all if he mean to take her to dwell with him), but in *seducing* and *inticing* her, can have no such *holy sober* notions in his head, as you plead for; but as he first had an intercourse with her from a love of variety, so now he takes her as a punishment to which he is condemned by law, for having basely gratified his lust, though perhaps like Amnon with Tamar *his hatred of her is greater than the love wherewith he loved her.*

But whatever might be the reason why the all-wise God ever permitted polygamous marriages among the Jews, he has now under the gospel, as will yet more clearly appear, thought proper absolutely to prohibit them, and therefore to attempt their restoration under the notion of *any holy or sober use of them,* is to set up our own judgment against the infinite wisdom of God himself.

As to what you would urge from the example of Abraham, it is certain, that no man since his time could be in his particular situation, for to him was the promise made, *that his seed should be as the stars of heaven for multitude:* And it is very observable, that the father of the faithful took unto him Hagar the Egyptian (who was a type of the Jewish church), at the particular instance of Sarai his wife, when both he and she supposed that *the Lord had restrained her from child-bearing*. A plain proof that he had more an eye to the fulfilment of God's promise, than to the gratification of his own lust; till therefore we find ourselves exactly in his predicament, we had better let his precedent for Polygamy entirely alone.

Were you to ask me how all the evils of fornication, uncleanness, seduction, and adultery might be cured? I would answer the question, by inquiring how you would attempt

attempt to cure the depravity of fallen man? which can never be effected by adding the evil of Polygamy to those before mentioned, but by enforcing the divine law; but what law? not the judicial law of Moses, which you produce, but the holy spiritual law of God. Let the ministers of the gospel open and apply this law in its extent and purity, to the consciences of sinners, to shew them their transgression and their helplessness, and then let them freely preach Christ as the only remedy, both from the guilt and dominion of sin. This will be truly answering God's own purpose both in the temporal or typical punishments under the law, which are now abolished, and were then *only a shadow of things to come*; as also under the gospel, the rejectors of which *shall be punished with everlasting destruction from the presence of the Lord, and the glory of his power*; whilst those who truly believe it, and embrace it *in the light and in the love of it*, shall *receive the end of their faith, even the salvation of their souls*. This preaching of the moral law for the discovery and conviction of sin, and preaching the gospel of the free grace of God as the only method of salvation *from* sin, will do more in *one year* for the cure of seduction, adultery, fornication, and lasciviousness in all its branches than a thousand treatises upon Polygamy, though they should have been *twenty years* in compiling.

STILL once more let us suppose your scheme established by the legislature just as you would have it. Very soon after, my dear friend to his own great grief, reads the following paragraph in the Morning Post.

" Last night lady A——, wife of Sir
" Thomas A——, Bart. was found hang-
" ing in her own dressing-room, in ——
" Square. The cause of this dreadful ca-
" tastrophe is supposed to be as follows:
" About a week ago, Miss B——, daugh-
" ter of William B——, Esq; went off
" from the masquerade at Carlisle House,
" with Sir Thomas A——. Next day,
" her mother, Mrs. B——, hearing that
" she was at Sir Thomas's house, came to
" her

"her in the utmost distress, and interro-
"gating her on the cause of her conduct,
"she replied with great pertness, that nei-
"ther she nor Sir Thomas had done any
"thing they need be ashamed of, or that
"was not authorized both by the law of
"God and the law of the land. Sir Tho-
"mas A—— was the *man of her choice*;
"she had *surrendered up her person* to him,
"she was now his wife without any more
"ceremony whatever, with him she meant
"to continue *all her days*; and he might
"take to himself twenty more young la-
"dies in the same way, if he thought pro-
"per; she had no right to controul him,
"whilst the divine law, as well as the law
"of the land, which had lately passed the
"King, Lords, and Commons, in favor of
"Polygamy, was now in full force."——
"Heavens, child! (cried the affrighted pa-
"rent) do you know that Sir Thomas
"A—— is already a married man, and
"has a virtuous good wife of his own;
"and that what you have done will cer-
"tainly break her heart?—Know it, yes,
"very well, but what is that to me? (re-
"plied

"plied Miss) Ought I to pretend to be "wiser than God ? or to wish to see hu-"man inventions, superstitious ceremonies, "and priest's marriages adopted, instead of "what he himself has appointed ? No, no, "I have now done with all these fooleries, "since Sir Thomas A—— has put into my "hands a very fine book with a very hard "name, upon these subjects; and if every "body was to do as Sir Thomas and I "have done, seduction, fornication, and "adultery, would soon be banished out of "the kingdom; and to tell you the truth, "as soon as I hear that the book is "*abridged*, I intend to buy an hundred to "disperse among the poor by way of cha-"rity." This answer of the young lady, had such an effect on the wretched mother, that she was carried home in a chair and expired the same evening; so that lady A—— and Mrs. B——, have both lost their lives by this unfortunate marriage.

Now I do not say that such a case ever will happen; but this I must say, that all this, and much more of a like sort might
happen

happen if your plan were to pass into a law, for in the whole of this transaction, whatever motives might influence either the supposed characters of Sir Thomas A——— or Miss B———, neither the one nor the other have acted in the least tittle contrary to what your own book authorizes: and feigned (God be praised) as the case is, yet I thought the introduction of it very allowable, by way of contrasting some of those melancholy pictures, which you have drawn and hung out to public view on the other side. I may add, that it is repaying you in your own coin, for as you have ransacked old newspapers to point out the blessings of Polygamy *in futuro,* it is very fair that I should have recourse to what we may naturally suppose will be the language of those papers, in order to point out the curses which will attend the monster when brought forth: and indeed, to shew the wisdom of that law which makes every Polygamist suffer death as a felon; but for which punishment you yourself have made the best apology, by wishing it were still to be put in execution upon the adulterer: therefore you cannot

cannot blame thofe who looking upon Polygamy and adultery to be fynonimous terms, have thought fit to inflict a fentence on the former, which you judge to be merited by the latter.

Such are a few of the flagrant mifchiefs which muft inevitably attend the introduction of Polygamy into this land, and yet they are but a few, in comparifon of others which muft ftrike the mind of every thinking perfon. For God's fake therefore, my dear friend, confider the dreadful licentious tendency of your affertions. Should one man defile another man's wife, you feem to lament that our laws do not punifh him with death; but if he intice or debauch a thoufand virgins, and afterwards take them to live with him, and call them by the name of wife, there is no harm done. It is a perfect marriage in the fight of God. There wants no human ceremony to complete it. The man is guilty of no fin. The woman, or rather each woman, is perfectly innocent; fhe has *furrendered up her perfon to the man of her choice*, and it would
be

be the highest impropriety to *upbraid* her with the name of a *whore*.

If such reasoning be not (though I grant most undesignedly) to give a sanction to fornication and lewdness, I know not what is; and if I have or shall prove the absolute unlawfulness of Polygamy in the course of this work, you yourself must be of the same opinion; at present however, you are not of that mind, having given us a pretty strong proof of your sentiments on this point, in the case of a certain noble earl and the late unfortunate Miss R——y, whom you positively affirm, that the Rev. Mr. H———— ought to have looked upon as the earl's wife: and no doubt his lordship is much obliged to you for the healing plaister which you have administered to him: and he may now console himself with another Miss R——y, and another yet, if he thinks proper; without sin on his part, or cause of shame in that of the females.

Permit me now to state a case, and to ask your opinion on it.

As

As a magistrate, it may have frequently happened that a single woman has come before you to filiate her bastard child on a married man. Now I should be glad to know, what you would say to the parties on such an occasion? From your character as a minister of the gospel, we may reasonably suppose, that the man and the woman would expect you should not only enforce the statute *concerning bastards begotten and born out of lawful matrimony*, but that you should also add some seasonable advice and reproof concerning the sin they have been guilty of. But how great must be their surprize, if you were to address the two persons before you in the following language; and yet if you are true to your own principles, I see not what other you can make use of.

" My friends, why are you uneasy? You
" have neither of you done any thing
" wrong in the sight of God, or that you
" need be ashamed of; so far from it, you
" have fulfilled the divine command, *in-*
" *crease and multiply*; and it is a scandal
" to our laws, that this poor girl should be
" deemed

"deemed a whore. Besides, I pronounce
"you to be useful members of the com-
"munity, by the encouragement you have
"given to population.

"Go your ways therefore, take the wo-
"man to live with you, and continue to
"act together as you have done. You are
"truly man and wife in the sight of God,
"without going through the forms of that
"superstitious ceremony which we call *ma-*
"*trimony*; though we clergy are obliged to
"trudge through the farce of reading, what
"is called, the church service, before the
"parties can be joined in law."

As I hear a third volume of *Thelyphthora* is soon to make its appearance, your sentiments on the case in question, will no doubt oblige the public.

You would appear to disapprove the practice of *keeping mistresses*; but I beg to inquire where is the harm of this according to your system, if the man who keeps the woman be the first who had intercourse with her?

her? You say, in such case, *he may not put her away all his days.* It seems then the sin is in *putting her away,* not in *keeping her*; for he sins not at all whilst he cohabits with her; all that time she is *his wife:* yet if he puts her away, I hardly know whether you would denominate her his wife or his mistress, seeing it was only a *temporary intercourse* that he had with her; and indeed upon your plan, it is almost impossible to say, who is a kept mistress and who a wife; for you have adjudged the late unfortunate Miss *Ray,* to be the wife of the first Lord of the A———y; and you say that the Rev. Mr. H———n, ought to have been taught to have looked upon her as such.

When that amorous Prince, Charles the Second, lay on his death-bed, before the Jesuits laid hold on him, he was attended by the pious Bishop *Kenn,* when the exemplary prelate exhorted him to put away his mistress, the celebrated *Nell Gwynne* [Z], and

[Z] I am not quite certain whether Eleanor Gwynne or the Duchess of Portsmouth, was at that time

and to be reconciled to his Queen. Had you, my good friend, been called to the dying Monarch, inſtead of the Biſhop of Bath and Wells, what advice would you have adminiſtered for his ſoul's health on that particular occaſion? The firſt piece of intelligence neceſſary to be obtained, would be whether any other man had been *one fleſh* with the favorite actreſs, previous to his Majeſty; in which caſe he was living in adultery with her, ſeeing ſhe was the true wife in God's ſight, of the firſt man who had been connected with her; but if his Majeſty *only* had been familiar with her, then ſhe was as much married to him by the divine law, as his own Queen was. How ſhall this difficulty be ſolved? Mrs. Gwynne alone can do it; and to her the reverend caſuiſt muſt put the deciding queſtion, and gather all the information he can relative to *the tokens of her virginity* before the King approached her. Mrs. Gwynne aſſures you, that no man whatever had ac-

---

time the reigning favorite of Charles the Second; but if I miſtake not it was the former; however that be, it makes no difference as to the caſe in hand.

ceſs

cefs to her perfon before his Majefty, and that ever fince fhe had been faithful to her royal lover. You anfwer (ftrictly according to the doctrine of *Thelyphthora*), " Then,
" Madam, you are his Majefty's *own* wife,
" and he is your *own proper* hufband, ac‑
" cording to the primitive inftitution of
" marriage, notwithftanding the ceremony
" which has paffed between him and his
" prefent confort, and notwithftanding no
" fuch form by a prieft has ever exifted
" between you and him: therefore, if his
" Majefty fhould recover from this illnefs,
" he would fhew himfelf a very wicked
" man in not living with you as he has
" done; and you Mrs. Gwynne, would be
" equally finful, if you did not continue to
" grant his Majefty every indulgence he
" requires at your hands. My advice there‑
" fore in this matter, for the prefent eafe
" of the King's confcience, and for his
" everlafting welfare, is this; that if it
" pleafe God to raife him up from this bed
" whereon he now languifhes, you both
" continue to give yourfelves up to the *holy*
" and *fober* embraces of each other, in

which

" which may you *be fruitful and multiply;*
" and may thousands of others, influenced
" by your virtuous examples, instead of
" *pretending to be wiser than God;* go on
" to follow those bright examples, till for-
" nication, adultery, and every species of
" lewdness be banished from this guilty
" land, which has forsaken the divine au-
" thority, and substituted human devices
" and superstitious ceremonies in its
" stead."

Is there a syllable in all this, which you as his Majesty's *spiritual guide* might not, nay *ought* not, upon your principles to have said upon the occasion?

Your definition of a whore is confined to one " who prostitutes herself to differ-
" ent men as lust or gain may induce her,
" *without design of marrying them.*" But I am quite at a loss to know what you mean by " *marrying them;*" do you suppose the woman to be unmarried, till some outward ceremony has passed? Can the *magic* words of a priest make her more a wife or less a whore

whore than she was before? if so, you throw down at once the whole structure you have been raising. If you choose to abide by your own assertions, you must avow that she was married to the first man with whom she *became one flesh*; and therefore she must necessarily commit adultery with all others she becomes afterwards connected with: so that I may venture to affirm, that according to your ideas of marriage, fornication cannot exist. I grant however, that the above is a true definition of *a common strumpet*; but whoredom, if scripture be our guide, might be committed even under the Mosaic dispensation, when any unmarried woman or widow, had intercourse with only one man, who was not her lawful husband; as is clear from the case of Tamar; for we read *Gen.* xxxviii. 24. *It was told Judah, saying, Tamar thy daughter-in-law hath played the harlot; and also behold she is with child by whoredom.* But according to your idea and definition of a whore, no man whatever had a right to say so. Suppose she had *surrendered up her person to the man of her choice,* whether

she

she were virgin or widow, or whether he were married or unmarried, she had done nothing that was forbidden, and therefore ought not to be stigmatized with the disgraceful appellation of a whore. It is true indeed, Judah took her for a common harlot, and he went in unto her as such. But this alters not the case, for they who *told Judah that she was with child by whoredom*, knew nothing of this intercourse, nor how it was obtained; and therefore the fact stands on record, as full proof that when any woman in Israel who had no husband proved to be with child, she was as much deemed an whore, as we should judge her to be one in England.

I must also observe, that neither Judah nor his friend Hirah, the Adullamite, seem to have thought it at all extraordinary, that they found an harlot sitting by the way side; nor did the men of whom *Hirah* inquired concerning her, express any astonishment at his question, as if some new thing had happened in Israel; but they simply made answer, that they did not see her; which circumstance,

cumſtance, beſides the frequent mention we have of harlots and adultereſſes in the Old Teſtament, and the cautions given to avoid commerce with them, as alſo the complaints of the prophets, that the people *aſſembled themſelves by troops in the harlots houſes, and were like fed horſes neighing after their neighbours wives,* carry pretty flagrant proof that adultery and whoredom were much more common in Judea, than you would have us believe, and that conſequently Polygamy was no ſpecific againſt either.

It has been urged, that if Polygamy be forbidden, ſome of the eminent Old Teſtament ſaints lived and died in adultery. It might with as much truth be objected, that if it be now unlawful for neareſt relations to marry, the immediate deſcendants of Adam and of Noah lived and died in inceſt; or if it be now wrong for a man to marry his brother's wife, it muſt have been ſo in all ages of the world, and under all circumſtances, ſince ſin can never alter its nature.

It

It will readily be granted that sin cannot alter its nature, and that God cannot alter *his* nature as bearing an everlasting hatred against sin. But then what is sin, but the trangression of the law of God? And what is the law of God, but the transcript and declaration of the will of God? And if God permit that at one time which he prohibits at another, the same act will be no sin when he allows it, which will be sin when he forbids it.—When Jael wife of Heber the Kenite, slew Sisera, the captain of Jabin's host, by driving a nail into his temples whilst he was asleep in her tent, she committed no sin, because she acted under the immediate direction of God; but had Jael done this without that direction, she had been guilty of the basest treachery and murder. Had Joshua when he conducted the Israelites to the promised land, acted by his own authority in burning the cities, slaying the inhabitants young and old, and even hanging five kings at once, after making his captains put their feet upon the necks of those kings, he would have been one of the most impious and arbitrary tyrants that the sun ever beheld; but by acting by the express warrant of Jehovah, in driving out and consuming the idolatrous nations, he had power to command that sun to stand still upon Gibeon, and the moon in the valley of Ajalon, whilst he completed his slaughter on the combined armies of all the kings of the Amorites, *Joshua* x. *throughout*.

But after all, suppose I cannot reconcile this difficulty to my own apprehension: suppose I am fearful of saying that Polygamy was no sin under the Old Testament, and am also fearful of asserting that Abraham, David, and others, lived and died in adultery; still why cannot I content myself with what is plainly revealed, and leave it to God to clear up the justice and equity of his own dealings with the children of men? Secret things belong unto him. Infinite wisdom has its own reasons for whatever it does, and will be accountable to none. Whatever be dark, this is certain, that God thought fit to *permit* Polygamy under the law: but permission does not by any means

means imply approbation; nay, God often permits that which from the very holiness of his nature is his abhorrence. On the other hand, it is equally certain, that God has thought fit to prohibit Polygamy under the gospel; and therefore though permission may well enough accord with disapprobation, yet prohibition and approbation are so far from agreeing, that they cannot stand together.

LET us now in as few words as possible, consider all the proof you attempt to bring from the Old Testament in favour of Polygamy, and the whole amounts to this: That in *no case* it was commanded or enjoined; in some cases it was permitted; but whether this permission ever amounted to approbation, remains still to be ascertained. It is true, you have brought some texts of scripture in defence of what you have advanced; but in none of these you have attempted to prove any thing beyond an allowance of Polygamy, except in one, and that is *Exod.* xxii. 16. *If a man intice a maid that is not betrothed, and lie with her, he shall surely endow her to be his wife.* And even this single text will not bear you out, unless you can bring some better proof than you have done, that *a man* (which you have unwarrantably ventured to render *any man*) means a married man, at least a married man, as well as a single one; in which interpretation however, you have not only the general voice of commentators against you, but if scripture be allowed to be its own interpreter, the voice of God himself, in that remarkable text which you have bestowed much pains to get over, *Lev.* xviii. 18. *Thou shalt not take a wife to her sister, to vex her, to uncover her nakedness, beside the other in her life time*; which those who have the most critical knowledge of the Hebrew, interpret as in the marginal reading, of not taking one wife to another, for which they have certainly very good authority, since the word which we translate a *sister*, is rendered *another*, in other parts of scripture.

The utmost therefore, which you have proved from the Old Testament, is a *permission*

mission of Polygamy among the Jews, not without much difficulty in getting over several texts, which at least seem very unfavorable to it, particularly that noted passage, *Mal.* ii. 14, 15, 16. which I shall give at length. *Yet ye say, Wherefore? because the Lord hath been witness between thee and the wife of thy youth; against whom thou hast dealt treacherously: yet she is thy companion, and the wife of thy covenant. And did not he make one? Yet had he the residue of the Spirit: and wherefore one? that he might seek a godly seed. Therefore take heed to your spirit, and let none deal treacherously against the wife of his youth. For the Lord, the God of Israel saith, that he hateth putting away, &c.* &c. Though it be certainly a humiliating circumstance for an author to confess himself ignorant of a language, the knowledge of which is in a degree necessary for the carrying on of a controversy in which he is engaged, yet rather than strut about like Æsop's daw in borrowed plumes, I will freely and ingenuously own myself incapable of examining into your Hebrew criticisms on the foregoing text, which I am

the

the more sorry for, as from the awkward or rather round-about explanation you have given of the passage, I am led to suspect that you have not faithfully delivered the mind and will of God revealed in it, particularly in those words, *Did not he make one?* i. e. as I always understood by comparing it with the context, " Did not he make the husband and wife one, by uniting them in so near a relation, that they two should be considered as one flesh ?"—But what is your sense of the words—*Did not one make? Or did not one God make or create both you and your wives?* Vol. I. p. 139. But whether you, or whether all " *the commentators that have followed one another like sheep,*" be in the right in the explanation of this clause, it is certain that if the whole three verses taken together, do not contain any absolute command that one man should have only one wife, it seems at least taken for granted, since there is mention made only of one man and one woman as united together in the nuptial bonds—and stiled, *thee and the wife of thy youth*, against whom the husband is cautioned *not to deal treacherously.*

Be assured, that I am as much against pinning my faith on the sleeves of commentators, as you can be; but yet I cannot help thinking, that there are many among them, who for learning, extensive knowledge, sound judgment, integrity and humility, are not at all inferior to those who affect to undervalue them. I am also persuaded, that though the knowledge of the original scriptures be very useful, yet that no point of real importance either to the faith or practice of a Christian depends upon, or requires a great skill in criticism. The gospel is preached to the poor, and the Lord knew, that comparatively few of his people would be deeply versed in languages.

I further beg leave just to observe, that though you profess most strongly to decry all human authority in general, because the current of it is against you, yet you are happy to make the most of every scrap and shred of it, when it is at all in your favor: I allow, that there is great danger in setting too high a value on any human authority whatever;

whatever; yet human authority where it keeps its proper place of subordination, is not without much use even in the investigation of divine truth: therefore where faithful ecclesiastical historians, fathers, and commentators, above all where the noble army of martyrs, and the holy church universal throughout the world, are and have been agreed in any point of doctrine from the first establishment of Christianity; though I am far from saying their testimony is infallible, yet I must say it is not to be lightly regarded, especially ought no one man without much fear, diffidence, and caution to set up his own judgment against so great a cloud of witnesses. We generally find that error and high self-confidence go hand in hand, whilst modesty and humility are the inseparable companions of truth. *The meek will he guide in judgment; the meek will he teach his way.* Psal. xxv. 9. When Thuedas arose, he *boasted himself to be somebody* [A], but Paul stiled himself

[A] Acts v. 36.

the chief of sinners, and less than the least of all saints.

After all, you will have no occasion to blame me for making too much use of human authority, as throughout this piece, I do not recollect that I have made one quotation, but what comes directly from the fountain of truth, *the word of God.*

But how have you succeeded when you come to the New Testament? All here is negative proof indeed; for with all your partiality to Polygamy, I bear you witness, that you have not even made the attempt of pressing a single text into your service. All you have done, all you could do, all you have endeavored to do, is to shew that the New Testament writings, allowing you your own interpretation of them, *may be* so explained, as not to forbid Polygamy; but not so much as one text is offered to prove even the permission of it.——Your grand argument is brought up again, again, again, and again, that if God allowed Polygamy under the Old Testament, it cannot be sinful

sinful under the New; and proceeding upon this most erroneous hypothesis, you bend and strain every scripture which stands in your way, till you have silenced them from speaking what they really do speak, and have made them speak just what you would have them speak. But whilst such bold liberties as these are taken with the blessed word of God, can we wonder that the doctrine of transubstantiation, or any other popish absurdities are swallowed down? Nay, are we to be astonished at the folly and enthusiasm of one in this kingdom, who some years since (you remember well the fact) declared he should never die, but should be translated as were Enoch and Elijah. Had any one reasoned with him on his delusion, might he not have said, "I see that two of the Old Testament saints were translated, therefore translation was then agreeable to the mind of God, the scriptures of the New Testament are intirely silent on this head; they leave the matter just as they found it, therefore, why may not I expect translation as well as

" as Enoch and Elijah?"—Indeed I think not only tranflation, but navigation, fortification, or any other *ation*, might as readily be proved from the New Teftament as Polygamy; befides, that to prove a doctrine from the New Teftament, which you yourfelf allow is not once mentioned in it, is I apprehend rather an odd manner of proving.

HAVING now, I hope, in fome meafure cleared the way before me, by removing many falfe ideas and mifconceptions, by which you ftrongly incline your readers in favor of your fyftem, and indeed in a manner try to frighten them into a perfuafion that the whole Chriftian world has hitherto been in darknefs, both in principle and practice, on the fubject in queftion, and that every interpreter of God's word who preceded you, has only been ringing poor Whittington's bells in their ears, to prevent their hearing diftinctly, what God fpeaks to them in his own written word; I fhall now endeavor by the help of God, to confider sider as briefly as possible, the plain obvious meaning of some texts of scripture in the New Testament, by which you attempt to support your cause, though I believe you will not deny but you have met with hard work before you took your leave of them.

The first text I mention is that, *Matt.* v. 28. *I say unto you, that whosoever looketh on a woman to lust after her, hath committed adultery with her already in his heart.*

Without the least proof as I can see in your favor, you insist upon it, that the word *woman* here must mean a married woman. But why so? Is there nothing improper in a man, whether married or single, lusting after any single woman or widow? None at all upon your system, if he means to make them his wives. But certainly you will not deny that the Greek word γυνη *mulier*, means any *woman* in general, married or unmarried, as much as the word ανηρ, *vir* means any man in general; and therefore to confine it to a married woman is to

make

make a limitation to serve a purpose, where God himself has made none [B].

Still further does this perversion of scripture appear, in your comment on that important text, ver. 32. of the same chapter. *I say unto you, that whosoever shall put away his wife, except it be for fornication, and shall marry another, committeth adultery: and whoso marrieth her which is put away, doth commit adultery.*

What labor and pains have you bestowed, to convince your readers that the word αλλην, *another*, means another man's wife, who

---

[B] My dear friend in his elucidation of this text, in order to evade its force, observes, that if by a woman *here* be meant *any woman*, then a man may commit adultery by looking at his own wife. At first I really felt myself hurt at the thought, that one for whom I have so high a regard, should descend to such low chicanery, but I presently recollected, *that he had been bred to the bar*, and therefore passed it by with a smile.

But the manner in which he speaks of *spiritual expositors* in the same place, instead of a *smile*, occasioned *a shake of the head*.

has

has been divorced from her husband, though the word is as general as constant usage can make it, and means any other woman, whether maid, widow, or wife. But then this plain reading of the text, for it requires no elucidation, would at once overthrow the doctrine of Polygamy; and cut up by the roots your new definition of adultery, by proving that a married man *may* commit adultery with a single woman. You are rather aware indeed of the tautology which you put into our Saviour's mouth, by your interpretation of this text, but still you try to get over it at all events. Let us render it as you would have it. *I say unto you, that whosoever shall put away his wife, except it be for fornication, and shall marry another* [that is say you, the wife of another man] *committeth adultery, and whoso marrieth her which is put away,* [who must still be the wife of another man] *committeth adultery.* Such is the tautology, not to say nonsense, which you make to proceed out of the mouth of him *who spake as never man spake*; whereas, take the words in their plain easy signification, and he that runneth

runneth may read, and come to the true fenfe of them. The paffage is mentioned by three evangelifts, and twice by St. Matthew; only in St. Mark it ftands double, and the crime is recorded as reciprocal on each fide. *Whofoever fhall put away his wife, and marry another, committeth adultery againft her. And if a woman fhall put away her hufband, and be married to another, fhe committeth adultery.* Now I would obferve, that the word *another* in the latter verfe, is the very fame in the original, when it relates to the man, as the word *another* is in the former verfe, when it relates to the woman, where you fay, it muft agree with the antecedent fubftantive γυναικα, *wife,* only differing in gender; fo that if we admit your conftruction in the one cafe, we ought to do it in the other, and make the word αλλω agree with its antecedent fubftantive ανδρα *hufband,* and then the whole paffage will run thus. " Whofoever fhall put away
" his wife, and marry *another man's wife*
" committeth adultery againft her; and if
" a woman fhall put away her hufband,
" and marry *another woman's hufband,* fhe

H " committeth

" committeth adultery." The conclusion of which interpretation is this, that if any man put away his wife (except for fornication) and marry another single woman or widow, he commits no adultery; and if a woman put away her husband, and marry another single man or a widower, she commits no adultery.—Alas! what will not evasion fly to!

The liberty you take in changing the word αλλην for αλλοτριαν must not pass unnoticed. I have consulted all the three evangelists where the passage is recorded, and no such word is to be found: St. Matthew and St. Mark both have αλλην, and St. Luke alone uses the word ετεραν which is nearly the same as αλλην *another, any other woman;* but the word αλλοτριαν which you have introduced, means *belonging to another;* or when joined to γυναικα *the wife of another man.* Now can we suppose, that if our Lord wished to have his own meaning understood in this most important matter, he would have used an expression which was very liable to be mistaken, and have left it

to

to you or me to make an amendment in his language; by leaving out one word, and substituting another? but instead of speaking ambiguously, he has vouchsafed to give us one of the plainest expressions imaginable, and which in its easy literal sense is capable of no other construction than that which our translators have given us. Nor does your *facetious gentleman's* story of the *glass* and *leathern bottles*, at all make in your favor, but quite point blank against you; though I allow that a joke may sometimes tickle the fancy of the tired reader, and cause him to mistake witticism for argument. And here I may observe, that when you were entertaining us with the story of Harlequin getting into a quart bottle, (vol. II. p. 352.) you might have added, that he also jumped down his own throat, which was not only *advertised* at the same time with the quart bottle business about thirty years ago, but I myself saw it attempted at one of the theatres; though I must own with not much better success than a friend of mine attempts to prove, *that any woman whatever,*

whatever, means another man's divorced wife.

My friend would illustrate this by that text, 1 *Cor.* x. 19. ὑπο αλλης συνειδησεως which is translated *another man's conscience*; but the words are strictly *another conscience*; and the addition of *man's* is inserted by way of expletive, and because another conscience and another man's conscience are synonimous terms, seeing no man can have more than one conscience.—But this is no argument at all, why another woman must mean *another man's divorced wife*, unless you can prove that every woman living stands in that predicament.

But to return, You will say, that our Lord in this passage is not speaking of Polygamy, but only of divorce. True, the question put by the Pharisees, proves that he is speaking of divorce; but in so doing, he is naturally led to shew what that crime is, for which divorce is lawful, and this is adultery; which if there be any meaning in

in words, he tells us may be committed when any married man takes to himself any other woman besides his own wife, be that other woman as before observed, a virgin, a widow, or a wife. And if we consult the context, we shall perceive that in the reasoning which our Lord makes use of, in order to satisfy the inquiry of the Pharisees concerning divorce, he refers them to the original institution of marriage. *Have ye not read* (saith he) *that he which made them at the beginning, made them male and female, and said, for this cause shall a man leave father and mother, and shall cleave to his wife, and they twain shall be one flesh? Wherefore they are no more twain but one flesh. What therefore God hath joined together, let no man put asunder.* As if he had said, " Know
" ye not that when God created Adam and
" Eve, he made the one male and the other
" female, and ordained that they should
" be faithful to each other, and keep the
" marriage bed inviolable: from thence-
" forth therefore, the husband and the
" wife are no longer to be esteemed as se-
" parate persons, but though twain or two
" in

"in number, are one flesh in the sight of
"God; upon which account, a man must
"leave his father and his mother, and must
"cleave unto his wife, not only in body,
"but in heart and affection. Therefore
"ye Pharisees do greatly err, when you
"suppose that it is lawful for a man to
"put away his wife for every or for any
"cause; for though for the hardness of
"your hearts this practice was suffered by
"the law of Moses, yet from the begin-
"ning, when God first instituted the bond
"of marriage, it was otherwise, for he
"then made only one man for one woman,
"and one woman for one man, wherefore
"I now tell you, that whosoever putteth
"away one wife, and marrieth another
"woman in her stead, committeth adul-
"tery, and whoso marrieth her that is put
"away committeth adultery."

Certainly, no one can say, that this is any forced comment upon our Lord's words on this very important passage, but a plain easy paraphrase upon the text, which so far from countenancing, directly militates

tates against Polygamy, and actually condemns it as adultery.

After much pains indeed, to state a distinction between the husband and wife being *legally* two, and *numerically* two, you seem to wonder at what you call the legerdemain of those, who suppose that the husband and wife mean only two persons, or *two and no more*. But surely, the art of legerdemain is much more to be admired in him, who can change οἱ δυο they two, into they three or they four, just as he pleases, and who by the same art can reduce Solomon and his seven hundred wives into οἱ δυο *they twain*.

The apostle Paul alludes to that original text, *Gen.* ii. 24. in his Epistle to the *Ephesians*, ch. v. 31. where he is treating of the love and union which ought to subsist between the husband and the wife. *For this cause shall a man leave his father and his mother, and shall be joined to his wife, and they two shall be one flesh.* And then he adds, *This is a great mystery, but I speak concerning Christ and the church.*—Nothing

thing can be clearer, nothing more restrictive of one man to one woman, and one woman to one man, than these words of the apostle.—But my friend would draw a conclusion in his favor from this text, by observing, that the church or spouse of Christ, being made up of many members, and having only one husband, therefore the analogy between Christ and his church is much better supported by the Polygamist than by the Monogamist.—But he should recollect, that though the believers which constitute the spouse of Christ, are indeed *many* when considered *individually*, yet when considered *collectively*, in which light the scripture always does consider them, they are still only ONE BODY; unless therefore, my friend can prove, (what the amorous Polygamist would not wish him to prove) that a man may have three or four wives, and these wives have but *one body* among them, the argument on which he hangs his conclusion, is no better than a rotten rope, which being pulled too tight, snaps in the middle, *and down drops Polygamy*.

I intended in this place to have introduced a comment or paraphrase upon the whole seventh chapter of St. Paul's first Epistle to the *Corinthians*, but considering how much I had already said on that chapter a few pages back, let me only intreat the reader " to lay down my book and take " up a better," and let him turn to that chapter as it came in perfect purity out of God's own hands, unmixed by paraphrases, or unadulterated with human comments; and when he has read the whole of it throughout, let him cease to wonder if he can, that there ever existed a man of sense, learning, and piety, who could believe that chapter, and yet maintain Polygamy.

Suffer me however, just to ask a few questions on those words, *Defraud ye not one the other except it be with consent for a time.*

1. Can more than two persons possibly be included in those words, " *one the* " *other ?"*

2dly,

2dly, Is not the confent of the wife as much included as the confent of the hufband, in the apoftle's injunction?

3dly, Does not a hufband more effectually defraud a wife of the rights of the marriage bed, by taking another woman, than by continence? In the former cafe he defrauds her *pofitively*; in the latter only *negatively*.

4thly, Was there ever an affectionate wife in the world that would give her free *confent* to be fo defrauded?

Now remember my requeft, and read the chapter throughout with reverence and attention.

THERE is yet one text of fcripture, which as you feem to lay much ftrefs upon, I fhall beg particularly to confider. The words are found, *Tit.* i. 6. *If any* (i. e. if any elder) *be the hufband of one wife.* From hence you conclude, that as by the apoftle's direction the elders were to be chofen out of thofe who were hufbands of one wife, therefore there muft certainly be among the

the Christian laity many who had more wives than one. But we may just as well infer, that because the elder women were to be selected out of those who had each of them been the wife of one man, (1 *Tim.* v. 9.) therefore there were many other Christian women who had more husbands than one. The words directly answer to one another in both places. *The husband of one wife,* or *of one woman;* and the wife of one husband, or *of one man,* and the purposes for which they were chosen, were in many cases the same [C]; so that as you interpret the one text with regard to the woman, who was to be chosen as a deaconess from among the widows, that she must be one who had only been once married; so you must also interpret the other text which relates to the man, (whether priest or deacon) that he must be chosen out of such as had only been once married. —But you say that text, 1 *Tim.* v. 9. which relates to the widow, is in the past tense, *having been* the wife of one man,

[C] More particularly where the man was chosen to the office of a deacon. See 1 *Tim.* iii. 12.

whereas

whereas the text *Tit.* i. 6. is in the prefent tenfe, *if any* be *the hufband of one wife.* I anfwer, that if this had not been the cafe, the woman would not have been a widow, but a wife, whereas the choice was to be made, of fuch an one as *had been,* not of fuch as *then was,* the wife of one man, becaufe a married woman being in fubjection *to the law of her hufband,* and at his difpofal, could not fo properly attend to the affairs of the church, where fhe was to be employed in performing different offices of relief and kindnefs to the fick and diftreffed members of it, as a widow could: whereas the objection did not lie fo ftrongly on the man's fide, whofe province it is not to take upon him the care of houfhold matters: But ftill the difference of tenfe, makes no difference of fenfe, in the point before us, and therefore, what the paffage means in the one place it means in the other, viz. that both the man and the woman fhould only have been once married, that they might attend to the affairs of the church with lefs diftraction, by not being burdened with family encumbrances.———And here, I muft must further observe, that in paraphrasing on these texts, you have made some concessions which are not very friendly to the doctrine you espouse, I mean that of Polygamy; (for it evidently appears by the chain and connection of both your volumes, that this is the great *Diana* which you would set up, and for the sake of which the whole was written) for you grant that the man to be chosen to be a bishop or presbyter, ought not to have two wives at a time. But why not? can that be wrong under the gospel, which was right under the law? Is *Paul* come to contradict *Moses?* *Elkanah* the priest, notwithstanding he had all the duties of his office to attend to, had two wives at a time, and why may not any Christian priest or presbyter have the same? Thus ought you to reason, if you would be consistent with yourself, else you immediately destroy the building which you have all along been attempting to set up, " That whatsoever " God allowed under the Old Testament " dispensation, he cannot disallow under " the New." Your argument therefore, once more proves too much, and lays you

under

under the necessity either of allowing Polygamy on the woman's side, or of disallowing it on the man's: or otherwise, you are constrained to grant, that God for wise reasons has thought fit to forbid a plurality of wives to his ministers under the gospel, though he permitted it under the law. If you still urge that this prohibition was more especially confined to the distressed or infant state of the church, I will not dispute the point with you; but this is a further argument in my favor, and verifies my assertion, " That God as sovereign of his
" creatures, has full right to disallow and
" forbid at one period, what he allows and
" even commands at another, according as
" he sees fit that times and circumstances
" should alter; and that still God changeth
" not, neither in his own nature, nor in
" his will, since the one great end he has
" in view is his own glory, and the good
" of his church and people."

HAVING endeavored to restore several texts of scripture to their original meaning, which appeared to me to be manifestly distorted

torted by your explanation of them in favor of Polygamy, I proceed to make a few short observations on what you have said more particularly relative to marriage.

Most justly you condemn the church of Rome for her unscriptural injunctions of celibacy, as well as some of the primitive fathers, for their unauthorized declamations against second marriages: but it is easy to conceive, that these errors might be adopted, by extending those passages of scripture to after-periods of the church, which were only designed for the primitive and distressed ages of it, which will therefore admit of some excuse, though not for the church of Rome, yet for the earliest fathers who lived in those ages, for what they have advanced in those points; and certainly our Lord and his apostles, more especially St. Paul in the seventh chapter of the first Epistle to the *Corinthians*, do under particular circumstances, and where the case of the parties will admit of it, give the preference to a single life, and encourage widows and widowers not to embark again in the married state,

state, without they find themselves under the necessity of so doing.—Some humble apology therefore may be made, though not for Rome herself, yet for the primitive fathers who have written such extravagant encomiums of virginity, by reflecting, that they lived in those very times for which all those texts which speak in favor of it were intended; but although in after-ages *superstition* so far kept the throne, that she attributed I know not what merit to an unnatural celibacy, and even ordained sanguinary laws for the punishment of priests who should marry, in direct defiance of God's great command, *increase and multiply*; still this proves nothing but that superstition is, and always will be superstition, but it adds not the weight of a grain to your arguments in favor of Polygamy: on the contrary, I should not wonder, if it were to be urged against you, perhaps many years hence, "That amidst the various cor-
" ruptions and superstitions which from
" time to time infested the Christian church,
" relative to divorce, marriage, celibacy,
" &c.

"&c. at last in the eighteenth century, flourished one *Martin Madan*, a person of great learning, judgment, and piety, who being determined to run as far as he could from the Romish church in these points, leaped into the other extreme, and actually wrote two volumes in defence of Polygamy." But I hope the ecclesiastical writer will immediately add, that "being convinced of his error, he recanted it with true Christian candor and contrition of heart."

Whilst I am on this subject, I cannot help observing how repeatedly you have brought up that statute of Henry VIII. which enacted, that no priest should marry on pain of death. And what is the conclusion you wish to draw from it? Why, that from the unscriptural absurdity of that statute, a direct contrary one ought to be enacted, and that because no priest might then be permitted to marry *one* wife, now any layman at least, should have the liberty of marrying two or more; which is just as

I good

good reasoning, as if I were to say, that if that parliament had been absurd enough to pass a law that every priest should have his nose cut off, therefore another act ought now to pass, for any layman to have two or more noses [D]. Or because the French capuchin friar you mention told you, it was contrary to the rules of his order ever to wear a pair of shoes at all; therefore it was now proper and expedient for a man to wear two or three pair at once.

But leaving the fooleries and extravagancies of popery to those who choose to be

[D] So far is the credulity of popery from supposing that a priest may not well enough exist without a nose, that it can even believe a priest may live without a head. —Whoever has visited the convent of St. Dennis near Paris, has seen the image of that Saint in silver with his head in his own hands; and has been told with a very grave face, by the ecclesiastic who shews the treasures of the church, that St. Dennis (from whom the convent takes its name) having suffered decapitation for the sake of religion, afterwards took up his head in his hands, and carried it from Paris to the place where the monastery now stands, which if I remember right, is a distance of about six miles.

amused

amused with them, I pass on to a circumstance which you mention, vol. I. 212, *note*, concerning some of our principal reformers, at the head of whom you have deservedly placed that great champion of the Protestant faith, Martin Luther. I mean, " their " *unanimous* agreement at *Wittemberg*, that " it was not contrary to the divine law, " for a man to have two wives at once." On which authority you inform us, that *Philip, Landgrave of Hesse*, actually married a *second wife*, his *first* being alive.

The case of the *Landgrave* of *Hesse* was a very particular one, and is taken from an authority which you do not much choose to avow. If I judge right you have gathered it from *Polygamia Triumphatrix*, p. 554. A performance which I perceive has been of signal use to you. The fact was, that the wife of the *Landgrave* found herself for especial reasons incapable of cohabiting with her own husband, and he found himself under a scriptural necessity of avoiding celibacy. To descend to the *minutiæ* of this matter,

matter, would lead me into a diſſertation, which I am ſure the delicate reader would wiſh me to avoid: ſuffice it ſay in general, that they could not live together as man and wife. The caſe was referred to the conſideration of the proteſtant divines, among whom were *Luther*, *Melanchton*, and *Bucer*, who after great deliberation and caution and not without much diffidence, delivered their opinion, that under ſuch circumſtances, the Landgrave might be permitted to take another wife.

But though I have examined various parts of that laborious treatiſe (*Pol. Tri.*) I cannot any where diſcover the quotation you have brought and marked with inverted commas, as put by way of a queſtion, to the aforeſaid divines at Wittemberg, "Whether for a "man to have two wives at once was con- "trary to the divine law?" Nor do I ſee any thing of their *unanimous* anſwer, "That " it was not;" therefore I hope if you publiſh another edition of *Thelyphthora*, you will tell us from what ſource you have derived

rived your authority for this propofition to the divines, and their *unanimous* reply to it.

But furely Luther inftead of being that firm inflexible and fteady character he was ever efteemed to be, muft have been the moft pufillanimous, wavering, and inconfiftent of all mortals, if he had delivered the opinion you charge him with, if the circumftances of the cafe had not been very particular: for looking over *John Sleidan's* hiftory of the Reformation in Germany, in order to fee if any thing was mentioned there concerning the cafe you allude to of *Philip, Landgrave of Heffe*, though I met with nothing at all on that head throughout the whole book, yet I found the following remarkable paffages from a work of Luther's (which had the full approbation of Melanchton, Bucer, and the other proteftant divines) relative to the *Anabaptifts* of that time which will clearly fhew what was the opinion of thofe great reformers on the matter of Polygamy.

" The

"The evil Spirit who endeavors to de-
"ſtroy the Chriſtian religion, does not
"uſually make choice of Polygamy for the
"compaſſing his deſigns, he knows the in-
"famy and wickedneſs of ſuch a practice
"is ſo notorious that all men abhor it."

Again. "To marry as many wives as
"his lewdneſs has a mind to, can be the
"contrivance of none but ſome raw un-
"practiced devil."

Now from theſe extracts which I have tranſcribed *verbatim*, can any man in the world ſuppoſe, that *Luther*, *Melanchton*, and *Bucer*, at the very ſame period that they were condemning Polygamy in ſuch ſevere terms among the *Anabaptiſts*, were abetting and encouraging it in the *Landgrave of Heſſe?* The thought is ſo abſurd and extravagant, that it cannot be harbored for a moment: I would therefore humbly propoſe an amendment in your words, "this "proves what they thought" [viz. what *Luther*, *Bucer*, and *Melanchton* thought on
the

the matter of Polygamy] " but by no means that they thought *right*," and would infert in their ftead, " This proves what I would have them think, but by no means what they did think."

The above-named learned, pious, and faithful hiftorian *John Sleidan* giving an account of that peftilent fect called Anabaptifts, (which was totally different from thofe we now call Baptifts) tells us, that " they introduced Polygamy;" that *John* of *Leyden* their chief leader or king, commanded his twelve teachers to declare, " that a man was not obliged to confine " himfelf to one wife, but might marry as " many as he pleafed;" that thereupon " they harangued upon matrimony from " their pulpits for three days together; " foon after which, he (*John* of *Leyden*) " married no lefs than three wives."—That " moft of their party had no lefs than five " wives a man. That this impious wretch " who was their principal prophet, made one

" of

" of his wives kneel down and beheaded her
" with his own hands in the market place."

How am I grieved to find my worthy friend in such company! but indeed I can see no difference between his doctrine and theirs in the point of Polygamy, only that these people did not go such lengths as to take their wives before they were married to them by an external ceremony, whereas he explodes every thing of this sort as superstitious priestcraft.

WE differ very little if at all, in our sentiments on the marriage act. I have long considered it not only as most inimical to the interests of the nation, but as standing in direct opposition to those great commands of God himself, *Be fruitful and multiply. Those whom God hath joined together, let no man put asunder.*

Whether or no the mere intercourse of a man with a virgin constitute a marriage in the sight of God, I will not dispute with you.

you. Certainly, the man in such case, ought by the law of God, to make her his wife, as I have elsewhere observed: yet, I think it both a dangerous and an unscriptural position to say, that she really is his wife, independent of any law or ceremony whatever: which law or ceremony, however it may vary, according to times, circumstances, and the custom of different nations, is that solemn act of recognition which binds the parties together, making them one in a legal or political sense, and distinguishing their intercourse from that of brute beasts.

When God created our first parents in Paradise, he did not leave the man to take the woman to be his wife; but it is said, " *God brought the woman to the man.*" It is true, this act, form, or ceremony, call it which you will, was immediately between God and the parties, but still as our first parents alone were then created, it was the only one that *could* exist, and therefore your remark, that there was no *priest* on the occasion

casion was totally needless. To this form or ceremony however, most civilized and indeed even uncivilized nations seem to have had respect in their marriages from that time; and particularly our own church, by appointing a person who is usually called *the father*, (whether he be really so or not) to give the woman to the man, and I apprehend it is in allusion to this original form and institution, that the author of the *two sermons* so much quoted (and so much disapproved) by you, says, that the priest or minister now *acts in God's stead*, by receiving the woman from the father's hand, and delivering her to her intended husband: And I remember to have once seen a Jew's wedding at *Amsterdam*, where besides several other ceremonies, something of the same form was observed.

Here I must beg leave to state another case for your solution.

Suppose a woman to have been seduced by any man, whether married or single; or suppose she freely consents to give herself up for a time to any man; let us go further still, and suppose she were even a common prostitute: afterwards she is truly sorry and penitent for what she has done. Now ought such a woman to marry, (though I can hardly yet tell what you mean by the word) or must she for ever live unmarried? —If you say she may lawfully marry, then what becomes of *your own* definition of marriage, seeing by that definition she was in the sight of God, the true wife of the first man who was connected with her, and consequently if she have commerce with any other she is an adulteress, and the man with whom she has that commerce is an adulterer. If you say she may *not* marry any other man than him who was first connected with her, then in all probability you condemn the poor creature to all the temptations of a single life. So that in the one case lewdness and adultery, in the other celibacy and depopulation must be the effect of your system.

But

But I avoid any further disputation on this point, especially as you perfectly agree with me on the propriety and expediency of some outward recognition of marriage before the world, for the purposes of civil society; and as I heartily acquiesce with you, that whether this be done by an ecclesiastic, or by a justice of the peace, as it was in the last century, is of no essential importance.

Before I dismiss this subject, I cannot help taking notice, that under your chapter of marriage, you bring your favorite text to shew that nothing can be added to or diminished from a marriage in the sight of God, when there has been an act of union in the parties; which text however rather contradicts than confirms your assertion. The words are these: *If a man entice a maid that is not betrothed, and lie with her, he shall surely endow her to be his wife. If her father utterly refuse to give her unto him, he shall pay money according to the dowry of virgins*

gins [E]. But if she were really his wife before in the sight of God, by the act which had passed between them, it was not in the father's power to set up his own against the divine authority. So that either she was not his wife, or else the institution of God gave place to the will of the father.—This seems a clear proof that something else besides the mere knowledge of a woman's person was necessary to constitute a marriage under the Jewish law; not to mention that the words *he shall endow her to be his wife,* plainly intimate that she was *not* his wife till such endowment, notwithstanding the intercourse he had had with her.

The like may be said in the case of the woman of Samaria, who *had had five husbands,* and when our Lord held his conference with her, was living with one who *was not her husband.* But why not her husband, if the five first were dead, and the present one had taken possession of her per-

[E] *Exod.* xxii. 16, 17.

son?

son? Upon your plan, nothing else was necessary to make them man and wife: You therefore very unfairly, because without the least authority, suppose that one of the five first was then living.

Since I wrote the above, I have looked a second time into the Monthly Review for October 1780, and must acknowledge that what the Reviewers have said concerning our Lord's conference with the woman of Samaria, is so much more to the purpose, and so much better expressed than in my own words, that I beg to refer the reader to their remarks.

In the Review for the next month, is also a very satisfactory solution of the text, *Deut.* xxi. 15. *If a man have two wives, one beloved, and another hated, and they have born him children, both the beloved and the hated; and if the first born son be her's that was hated: Then it shall be, when he maketh his sons to inherit that which he hath, that he he may not make the son of the beloved first-born before the son of the hated, which is indeed the first-born: but he shall acknowledge the son of the hated for the first-born, by giving him a double portion of all that he hath, &c.*

As our present translation of this passage coincides with Mr. Madan's opinion, he is happy to admit it; had it been otherwise, he would have sheltered himself under the wing of his favorite commentator *Montanus*, who renders the words, *cum fuerint viro duæ uxores*. *If there shall have been to a man two wives*; or *if a man SHALL HAVE HAD two wives*; by which version there is no proof at all that he had the two wives both at once. Nay, these words, her's that *was* hated (not that *is* hated) being in the past tense imply the contrary. But admitting that he had, still the text carries not with it the least glimpse of an approbation of Polygamy on God's part, but is merely directory of what shall be done with the children by each wife.——It is said, Exod.

Exod. xxii. 2, 3. *If a man shall steal an ox or a sheep and kill it or sell it, he shall restore five oxen for an ox, and four sheep for a sheep.* But we have just the same reason to say, that God approves of *sheep-stealing,* as that he approves of Polygamy, because in both cases he gives directions what shall be done: in the one case, the thief was to make restitution; in the other, the Bigamist was not to add one evil to another, by disinheriting the eldest son of the hated wife, and giving his substance to the son of the favorite wife.

I cannot take my leave of what the Reviewers have said on *Thelyphthora,* without remarking, that I think those gentlemen have born rather too hard on Mr. Madan, in supposing that he was guilty of any want of reverence either intended or not intended, *towards Christ or towards the sacred scriptures,* because he says, "that if it "could be proved that in any one instance, "Christ added to or diminished from the "law of God, by ordaining any thing contrary

trary to or inconsistent with it, it would be making him a greater impostor than Mahomet." I doubt not, but Mr. Madan so far from thinking that that such an expression might excite " *emotions of indignation or disgust,*" meant by this forcible language against the idea of setting Christ and the divine law at variance to shew his own high veneration for both.—And indeed when we consider that the apostle John testifying his zeal against infidelity, says, *he that believeth not God hath made him a liar,* I think Mr. Madan's mode of speech is very justifiable on scripture authority.. Upon which account I should hope that the Reviewers, if they think there is any argument in what I advance, would candidly retract what they have said of my mistaken, but still worthy friend, (against whom they certainly have sufficient advantage in other points) for having uttered, what at the first perusal they judged to be *shocking* and *indecent,* and *tending to wound the ear of the modest and humble Christian.* But if they should still retain their opinion,

I hope they will pardon me for the liberty I have taken in endeavoring to vindicate one for whom I profess a sincere regard, so far as I believe his intention to have been good, and his words capable of a favorable construction.

Still another observation occurs to me on the text, *Exod.* xxii. 16, 17. which being nearly the same with that, *Deut.* xxii. 28, 29. I shall just mention what I have to say on them both together in this place, though perhaps I should have been rather more methodical in doing it in another. I have before remarked, that these texts rather contain a part of the judicial law, in the midst of which they stand recorded, than of the moral; and shew that the command of God which enjoined, that *if a man had enticed a maid and humbled her, he should make her his wife, and not put her away all his days,* was rather intended as a punishment to be inflicted on the offender for his baseness and lewdness, than as a sanction given by God to Polygamy.—But
whether

whether this law was ever enforced when the man was a married man, remains yet to be proved. You have indeed taken much pains to demonstrate that *a man* here must mean *any man*, married or not married, because your system cannot stand without it: But if I allow this, how can you disallow that *a woman* means *any woman*, married or not married? and yet you absolutely refuse to grant this, in your interpretation of that text, *Whosoever looketh on* a woman *to lust after her, hath committed adultery with her already in his heart*; as also where it is said, *Whosoever shall put away his wife and marry another committeth adultery*. In both these instances you insist that *a woman* must mean a married woman only, because otherwise Polygamy cannot stand.

The more I consider the primitive institution of marriage, the more I am convinced that Polygamy is not less contrary to the law of nature, than to the law of God: for

I. One

I. One woman only was created and given for the use and comfort of one man, whilst that man and woman were in a state of innocence in Paradise; and it is the business of Christianity to call us back as much as possible to that state.

II. When God peopled the world a second time, after the flood, it was without Polygamy, four men and four women only, who were wives to Noah and his three sons, were commanded to go into the ark [F]; and from them was the whole earth peopled.

III. Without entering into a minute discussion of your calculations concerning the exact number of males and females which are born in different nations, I believe it is a matter generally agreed on, that the males throughout the world are nearly one fifth more than the females [G]; so that if Po-

[F] *Gen.* vii. 13.

[G] *Süssmilch* Provost of St. Peter's at Berlin, made a calculation some years ago, by which it appeared, that throughout the King of Prussia's dominions, there were about 105 males to 100 females.

lygamy

lygamy were univerfally practifed, numbers of women muft of neceflity go without hufbands, and thereby God's great defign of forming the fexes for each other, muft be fruftrated.

IV. If *no man can ferve two mafters, becaufe he will love the one and hate the other, or elfe he will hold to the one and defpife the other;* how much lefs can one man love, cherifh, and comfort alike two wives? This feems fo abfolutely impoffible, that I fee not how any thing like God's original appointment of marriage and the mutual happinefs of man and wife, can be maintained upon the principles of Polygamy; nay, fo far from it, that it appears to me, that the only happy marriages, or rather the leaft unhappy ones, muft be thofe where there is the moft indifference between the parties; for where there is true love and affection, jealoufy, if it finds ground to reft on, will be hard at work, and that being the moft tormenting of all paffions, whatever is the caufe of exciting it, had better be abfent than prefent, confequently the woman's hatred of her hufband would make her lefs miferable than her love for him.—For any one to affert that a woman may have a true love and affection for her hufband, and yet feel no jealoufy at feeing him attached and given up to another, is at once to prove himfelf totally deftitute of all fenfibility, and ignorant of all the workings of human nature.—If therefore no man can (as before obferved) *ferve two mafters,* there is ftill a greater impoffibility that one man fhould, in the fcriptural fenfe of the expreffion, cleave to more than one wife at a time, viz. in heart, fpirit, and affection, as well as by a bodily union. Of this you are fenfible, and therefore you would confine this *cleaving to the wife* merely to the latter, which certainly does not carry with it that purity of fentiment which the fcripture language means to convey, and which is well illuftrated by *cleaving unto the Lord:* i. e. having communion and fellowfhip with him; in which fenfe only the union between

tween the husband and wife is compared with that which subsists between Christ and his church.

In all these instances the law of God, and the law of nature are so blended together, that they cannot be separated.

I cannot come to a conclusion without making some few observations on the advertisement which immediately follows the title of your book. I mean not however to call in question what you say of the *importance* or of the *interesting* tendency of your TREATISE, nor whether you have indeed so mixed " the *utile dulci* as to have avoided that *tiresome dryness* which usually attends treatise-writing, and to have introduced *much variety of entertaining matter.*" This affects not the grand question at all: therefore you are to think of your THELYPHTHORA on these points, just as you please, and your readers will think of them as they please. What I object against in that

that advertisement, is a very positive assertion, which seems hung out in the frontispiece, in order to strike the reader with horror, and to prejudice him in your favor, that " in the eye of our municipal laws, " women are of less consequence than the " beasts of the field; for it is *less penal* to " seduce, defile, and abandon to prostitu- " tion and ruin a thousand women mar- " ried or unmarried, than to steal, kill, or " even maliciously to maim or wound an ox " or a sheep." In proof of this you refer to 22 and 23 Car. II. ch. 7, &c.—9 Geo. I. ch. 22.—I had like to have said, that there is a most palpable *falsity* in this assertion, but I will recall the word, and instead of *falsity* we will read *fallacy*. It is true, the above statutes make it felony to steal, kill, or maliciously wound an ox or a sheep, but what proof is this, that " women are of " less consequence than the beasts of the " field?" or indeed where is the analogy between our laws relative to the one and to the other, unless you can demonstrate from the acts which you have quoted, that it is less criminal to *steal, kill,* or *maliciously wound* a wife or virgin, than to *steal, kill,* or *maliciously wound an ox or a sheep?* Suffer me therefore to inform you, that the persons of all women are so amply protected by our municipal laws, and their chastity is held so sacred, that not only the violation of it against their will is death to the offender without benefit of clergy, but even an *attempt* to commit a rape, is punishable by one of the most ignominious sentences that can be inflicted, viz. standing on the pillory, and this protection is not only extended to a wife or a virgin, but even to the most abandoned prostitute; and if the female be under ten years of age, then, even though she should consent to the act, the corrupter of her is adjudged to forfeit his life.—Where the females are of marriageable age, whether they themselves be married or not, though they should have had an intercourse with any man by their freest consent, still such man is liable to be severely fined, and to pay damages in proportion to his ability to the father or husband of the

the woman. To all this may be added, that to keep a brothel is punishable by fine, imprisonment, or pillory, according to the sentence of the court before which the party has been tried and convicted.

It may indeed appear rather presumptuous for a country justice of the peace (and I confess, we are most of us a very blundering wrong-headed tribe) to pretend to remind you who are so well skilled in all parts of our constitution of these things; but as we ourselves are seldom above receiving our instructions from our clerks, and are ready to sign (without reading) whatever they put before us, I flatter myself you will not think I mean to call in question your knowledge of, or acquaintance with any of the established laws of the nation, because I just take the liberty of whispering in your ear, what our clerks so frequently do to us, " Perhaps your worship " does not *immediately recollect* that such " and such a statute says so and so".

After

After all, there are certain cases wherein we have reason to lament that our laws punish petty offenders with the utmost rigor, whilst the most notorious villains are suffered to go free. And yet it is not possible for the wisest legislature to guard against this, nor is it owing to any defect in our present system, that it is so. The cause of this evil lies in the corrupt state of human nature. The cure must be looked for only at the hand of divine grace. Among these is the punishing with death, the afflicted wretch who steals money, goods, or even meat to support life to the value of one shilling, whilst the far greater robbers who increase their hoards by exorbitant premiums and usury, or who borrow large sums, perhaps to the distress of many families, without prospect of payment, in order to support their own extravagance, cannot be laid hold on as criminals.—And yet what can be done in such a case? To form proper penal laws against the two latter of these characters would be exceeding difficult, and the execution of them

them still more so.—To repeal those already made, and to suffer poverty to be pleaded in behalf of theft or robbery, would immediately expose the persons and property of every man, to all the horrors of rapine and plunder: and you of all people living, would dread the enacting of any law for superseding or mitigating the punishment of offenders, as I have frequently heard you say, and perhaps very justly, that sparing so many thieves and robbers from the gallows, is the cause of their increase. We may invent remedies for such or such evils, and when we have invented them, they may turn out worse than the diseases they are meant to cure. Among these remedies is that of introducing Polygamy by way of preventing adultery and fornication; and it calls to my mind a story which the famed Voltaire once told me at Geneva, of a French clown, who jumped into a river in order to escape a shower of rain.

However,

However, that the doctrine of *Thelyphthora* does indeed tend to make *women of less consequence than the beasts of the field,* perhaps the following instance will serve to evince.

I am now for the last time to suppose Polygamy established by law in this kingdom; and I will also suppose that it has been so for about five or six years. My servant knocks at my study door, puts a paper into my hand, and tells me that a poor woman who is weeping in the passage with three young children, begs me to read it over; I find it to be as follows:

"THE HUMBLE PETITION OF
"Mary, wife of John Williams, sheweth, that your poor petitioner has been
"married to the said John Williams, a
"labouring man, for the space of ten years
"and upwards; that he made your petitioner a good and an industrious husband,
"and maintained his family very decently
"till about four years ago, when he married

"ried another woman, by whom he has
"two more children; and after that mar-
"ried a third wife, who has at different
"times beaten your petitioner, as alſo his
"ſecond wife, in the moſt barbarous man-
"ner, and turned us both out of doors:
"beſides that the wages, which the ſaid
"John Williams earned by his work, were
"but juſt ſufficient to maintain your poor
"petitioner and three children when he
"had no other wife; ſo that if your pe-
"titioner had not been turned out of the
"houſe, ſhe and her young children had
"no other proſpect but that of beggary
"and ſtarving, which ſtill your petitioner
"(by the grace of God) had rather ſubmit
"to, than to turn thief or proſtitute to
"ſupply her wants, which the ſecond wife
"of the ſaid John Williams has done.
"Your petitioner therefore humbly hopes
"that all good Chriſtians will pity her de-
"plorable ſituation, and that of her poor
"deſtitute infants, and your petitioner will
"as in duty bound ſincerely pray.

MARY WILLIAMS,
her + mark.

Now is this case at all unlikely to happen upon the introduction of Polygamy? Nay, is there not all the reason in the world to suppose, that if not exactly the same, yet similar cases of wretchedness must abound in every corner of the land? And surely, whatever is the cause of this abject distress, must be the means of exposing women and children to too much greater hardships and miseries than the beasts of the field are subject to.

ALTHOUGH I have the honor of standing in a two-fold capacity among those to whom your *Treatise* is dedicated, viz. as a governor of the Lock Hospital, and as a member of the Legislature; yet you will readily suppose from the foregoing pages, that I think it absolutely incumbent upon me in each of those capacities to express my intire disapprobation of that *Treatise*; *First*, as being totally repugnant to the scriptures of truth. *Secondly*, as being pregnant with the most pernicious consequences towards the state, and calculated (however unintentionally by you)

you) to multiply all that train of evils which it would speciously appear to redress or prevent. I assure you, dear Sir, not from hearsay evidence, but from certain knowledge, that the altercations, dissentions, and prejudices against religion, which Polygamy in embryo has occasioned at a considerable distance from the capital, not only in two counties which are contiguous to me, but in that most respectable and most indulgent county which I have the honor to represent, have run so high, that I should dread its introduction by law worse than if any member were to move for leave to bring in a bill for the establishment of the plague. And though I hope the real sense I have of the deficiency of my own abilities, will ever prevent me from giving the house much trouble by my loquacity, and though upon most occasions, I shall probably content myself with giving an honest independent *aye* or *no*, yet if your system were ever to become the object of the legislature (of which however I see not the least prospect), I am persuaded I should not be able

to

to contain myself, but should esteem it my most indispensible duty, to bear an open testimony against it in the senate, as well as from the press.

Though it be a matter of too much notoriety, that the author of *Thelyphthora* is a reigning toast among the jovial sons of pleasure at their clubs and taverns, yet I should not have mentioned this circumstance, but as it tends to demonstrate the character and stamp of those who wish well to Polygamy, by the establishment of which alone, the husband who is fond of variety, or the young debauchee who is yet unmarried, can hope to get possession of the persons of those women who otherwise would not consent to their solicitations, and this not merely without feeling their consciences checked for the sin they might otherwise think themselves guilty of, but all the while congratulating themselves, that they are discharging their duty as faithful servants of God, and good members of the community. Thus Polygamy is made the *dernier resort* of (otherwise despairing) lewdness, and even

even covers the vilest debauchery, under the sanctimonious *doublet* of obedience to the divine law, and utility towards the state; whilst those who disavow the principles and practice of Polygamy, are held forth as laboring under the disease of a scrupulous conscience, and as being fast bound with the shackles of ignorance, superstition, and priestcraft.

It is now time that I should put an end to this painful epistle, which though circumscribed within a much narrower compass, will I believe be found to contain a reply to every material argument you have made use of, at least so far as the doctrine of Polygamy is concerned.

It may indeed be objected, that an answer to two octavo volumes, cannot possibly be confined to the limits of a book not much larger than a pamphlet, but I am under the necessity of remarking that your whole Treatise would not greatly have exceeded the bulk of my letter, had it been freed from its multiplied repetitions, and had

had you omitted pages without number, which anſwer no other end than to bias the reader in your favor, but which in truth and reality, have juſt the ſame force in whatever cauſe they are brought to ſupport. I mean your cenſure of thoſe who obſcure or adulterate the pure word of God by ſuch comments of their own deviſing, as *error, prejudice,* and *ſuperſtition,* may direct, *adopting ſound for ſenſe,* ſetting themſelves up to be *wiſer than God,* walking in the ſteps of *Socinus, Mahomet* [H], and *Ce-*

[H] As this falſe prophet was the grand patron of Polygamy, he muſt feel himſelf very aukward at being ſo frequently introduced into the company of Monogamiſts, and would certainly be much more at eaſe among thoſe of his own ſentiments on this head.

The learned Mr. Sale, in his tranſlation of the Koran, p. 204, *note,* mentions that one of the great reproaches caſt on Mahomet by the Jews, " was on ac-
" count of the great number of his wives. For the
" Jews ſaid, *that if he was a true prophet, his care and*
" *attention would be employed about ſomething elſe than*
" *women and the getting of children.*—It may be ob-
" ſerved (adds Mr. Sale) that it is a maxim of the
" Jews that nothing is more repugnant to prophecy
" than carnality."

rinthus, and setting *Christ* and *Moses* at variance.

Now it is certain, that a writer usually makes more converts to his opinion by declamation of this sort, than by any other method, because it at once raises the indignation of the reader against such sophisticators of God's word, whilst it banishes all suspicion that the person who is expressing his abhorrence of their practice, is himself found to adopt it; yet by these means an easy way is made for the introduction of an author's sentiments into the mind which is already so strongly prepossessed in his favor.

Far, very far be it from me, to affirm that you have done any thing of this sort, in order to deceive or mislead the sincere inquirer after truth. I bear you witness, that the honesty and integrity of your heart set you quite above the reach of such unfair dealing: but an overweening attachment to a favorite notion, has led you to conclude, that whatever parts of God's word seemed

to

to militate against that notion, must have been hitherto misunderstood; and hence I am sorry to say, that you have compelled scripture to stoop to your system, rather than suffer your system to stand or fall by the decisions of scripture.

I know that you have complained heavily of the many letters of remonstrance which were sent you, before the publication of your book, to desire you to suppress it. I can only say, it is pity you did not attend to them; for if it be a received maxim, that *vox populi* is *vox Dei*, how much more *vox amicorum*, how much more yet, *vox Christianorum!*

I find by your preface, that you submitted the perusal of your manuscript to some *learned and pious friends:* though I dare not lay claim to either of these adjectives, yet I do lay claim to a very great share in the substantive, and therefore beg to assure you, that if I had had the honor of being ranked among those friends, so far from joining them in their approbation, I should
have

have been ready to have done what Mrs. *Ainsworth* is reported to have done by the manuscript of her husband's dictionary, just as it was ready for the press, viz. to have committed it to the flames, for no other reason, than because the good laborious man (who by the bye found one wife quite a match for him) had the misfortune to break one of her favorite tea-cups: but my conduct would certainly have proceeded from much better motives than that of revenge, viz. love to my friend, love to God, and zeal for the interests of the gospel.

I would wish to convince you; but if I cannot do this, be assured nothing is further from my thoughts than to offend you; and therefore if you have found any thing throughout this letter which you may think bears rather too hard upon you, let me intreat you not to look upon it as levelled against you, but what I am fully persuaded are the errors you hold.

With heart-felt grief, I see that some eminent and faithful ministers of the gospel have

have imbibed your sentiments, and are even earnest in the propagation of them, whilst others are secretly won over to them, but through fear of domestic uneasiness, or other motives, do not choose openly to avow them.

These things I *do* see; but how far the evil will yet spread, I cannot see. I trust however, that the firm conviction I have in my own mind, of the great impropriety of your having sent the *Treatise* in question abroad into the world, will plead sufficient apology for this public address, from one who has always esteemed it both an honor and happiness to subscribe himself,

 Rev. and dear Sir,
  Your most sincere
   and affectionate friend,
    RICHARD HILL.

P. S. Your *Treatise* had been published full half a year before I could persuade myself to read it, which will account for my having been so long in sending out my answer to it.

ADVERTISEMENT.

I THINK myself in a manner obligated to publish the following Letter, in order to convince the reader, that I used every method in my power to avoid this controversy, by trying to prevent my much esteemed Friend from sending abroad his *Treatise*; which I hope will plead my apology for any repetition or sameness of argument, which may appear both in the letter and in the address.

A LETTER

TO THE

Rev. MARTIN MADAN.

My very dear friend,

I WAS exceedingly concerned to hear a few days ago, from one who has a sincere regard for you, that you are going to publish a book upon the lawfulness of Polygamy. I remember to have often heard you deliver your sentiments on the subject to particular friends, but never could have imagined that you would have sent them abroad into the world; and now beseech you to consider well the tendency of such a step, before you advance any further. Even suppose all, and more than all you could wish to have effected by the publication; suppose you should convince thousands that they might, without sin, have more wives than one; what end will this answer? What good will it do you? What glory will it bring to God? What advantage will it be of to society? To say the least, it will take up a great deal of your time, which might certainly be much better spent. It can render no service to the cause of christianity, unless you can also prove that every additional wife will bring with her an additional stock of grace. And with regard to society, it is likely to bring with it an innumerable train of evils; and the more; as all the passions, lusts and corruptions of human nature, will be so strongly inclined to favor your doctrine, that they will unite all their force to proselyte the judgment; and then who shall dare to split the difference between two wives and two hundred? And if this be allowed on the man's side, you will not doubt but there are females amongst us to be found, who will plead for an extension

of

of the privilege to their own sex. I do not say this age is worse than former ones, but I fancy you will agree with me, that it is not much better, and that we do not live in times wherein it is necessary to help mankind to a sanction for taking more wives than one, especially when they are well tired of the first.

I should do you the highest injustice as a man of sense, and as a christian, to suppose you had not some good and useful design in view by this intended publication: Yet what that design may be, I cannot at all conceive: But I evidently discern the most dreadful and pernicious consequences, if you should make many or any converts to your opinion; and if you do not make converts, *cui bono scribere?* It is all lost labour and waste paper. In the church of God, many *may* be staggered and puzzled, many *will* be ashamed and grieved; and lifeless professors will be gazing about at the *Locke* and *Tottenham* for some new object of delight, that when they have lost every other mark of saintship, they may at least follow the examples of some Old Testament saints, in having plenty of wives and concubines. And now I am upon this point, I remember that my dear friend's grand argument in support of his doctrine was that when the scripture mentions the polygamy of the Patriarchs, they are never censured on this account. But does this prove that what they did was no spot in their characters, or that it was agreeable to the mind and will of God? This, I think, would be a dangerous position, and might be equally urged as a plea for Noah's drunkenness, or Lot's drunkenness and incest together; none of which sins are particularly reprehended in the persons of whom they are recorded. I would wave disputes how far the Jewish worthies (though saved by faith in the same Redeemer) fell short of the privileges of those who live under the clearer light of the gospel; but certainly you will allow there was a difference between them; the former *saw through a glass darkly, the times of reformation* were not fully *come:* And as in the matter of *putting away their wives,* God bore with them, *becaufe of the hardnefs of their hearts,* fo how far he might do fo in their taking a plurality of wives, is, perhaps, not for us to determine; but certainly *from the beginning it was not fo,* Adam had only his Eve, though from her the whole earth was to be peopled.

Till, therefore, it can be proved that Polygamy is allowed by the gofpel of Chrift, the example of believers under the legal difpenfation, will not fufficiently authorize the practice of it; and fo far from being allowed, it appears to me to be moft clearly forbidden; for if our bleffed Lord condemns the repudiating one wife and taking another, except for the caufe of fornication, it is the fame thing, as if he had faid in exprefs words, that a man fhould have only one wife at a time. And when St. Paul fays, " To " avoid fornication, let every man have his " own wife, and every woman her own " hufband," the certain conclufion to be drawn from the injunction is, that every man who takes any other woman, doth *not* avoid fornication, any more than the woman who takes any other man does. And indeed the whole 7th chapter of the first Epistle to the Corinthians, is founded on the supposition (as a matter taken for granted by the whole christian church) that the husband has or can have but one wife, any more than the wife can have but one husband. Do, my dear Sir, read and pray over the whole chapter, and surely conviction must accompany the word.

I must further remark, that the allusion which the Apostle draws between the marriage bond and the union which subsists between Christ and his spouse, or his body, the church, would be a very unjust one, and would fail in almost every instance, if believers might have more wives than one at a time; and instead of saying that " *they two* (the husband and wife) shall be one flesh," he ought to have left the matter more at large, and should have said, " *they three*, or *they four*, shall be one flesh," which carries an abſurdity and contradiction in the very mention. Neither could he with any propriety have exhorted " every man to love " his wife even as himſelf," as that would be confining that affection to one alone, which each wife had an equal right to ſhare in; but as he ſpeaks in the ſingular, and not in the plural number, this proves to demonſtration, that a plurality of wives was never thought of, much leſs allowed by this choſen veſſel.

But not to multiply ſcriptures, (though many more might be produced) conſider the judgment and practice of the whole Catholic church from the very beginning. Can any one example be produced of the toleration of Polygamy? On the contrary, have not almoſt all chriſtian nations, our own in particular, puniſhed it with death, as an heinous offence againſt the laws of God, and the welfare of ſociety?

But I will go one ſtep further with regard to the Old Teſtament ſaints; I will even

ſuppoſe

suppose that God allowed them a plurality of wives; still this will not prove the point that Polygamy is lawful to Christians; for the only standard of right and wrong is the command and will of God; and when God wills or commands a thing to be done, then the doing of it ceases to be sinful, though abstracted from that command, it might be a notorious act of wickedness. Thus it was no sin in Samuel to hew the king of the Amalekites in pieces; though if God had not willed and commanded it, Samuel had been guilty of a very abominable murder. So to marry the brother's wife, was forbidden by the Levitical law, as an incestuous commerce; yet when the brother died without issue, it was actually enjoined the next brother to marry the widow, and to raise up seed unto his brother; and if he did not do so, he incurred the heavy displeasure of God, as in the case of Onan. All I argue from these instances, is, that God, as sovereign of all men, has full right to permit or order that at one time, or upon one occasion, which he has an equal right to forbid at others;

others; and therefore that he might suffer that to be done for his own wife purposes by Abraham, David, &c. under the Jewish œconomy, *that made nothing perfect*, which now he has the same right to prohibit to believers under the meridian of the gospel.

But now suppose all these arguments (and I might produce many more) have no weight with you; still let me return to my former question, What good is your book likely to do? If it be not against the express laws of God, I am sure it is against the express laws of the land; and subjection to the powers that are, has always been your avowed principle. Why, then, would you deviate from it in the present instance, when in proportion to your known character as a minister of Christ, and to your abilities as a lawyer and casuist, your book is likely to create confusion in the state, as well as in private families? Can you pray for God's blessing on your undertaking? Will the completion of it bring you any comfort on your death bed? Who, think you, will be
benefited

benefited by it? Will the community, will individuals be the better for it? Probably the officers of Doctor's Commons may get more grist to their mill by the additional number of divorces it may occasion; (though by the bye, these gentlemen have tolerable reason to be satisfied in this respect) and probably the author of the trials for adultery, will soon extend his filthy pages from five volumes to fifty.

But I find I am extending my letter to a tiresome length. Bear with me, my dear friend, and forgive me this wrong; and if you still think I have been deficient in arguments, suffer me to supply the want of them by intreaties. I beseech you, therefore, by the mercies of God in Christ Jesus, that you will not send out under the sanction of your very respectable name, a book of such a dangerous tendency; and if you have any love for your christian friends, (which of all others, I have no reason to doubt) any concern for the glory of God, the peace of his church, your own reputation, and the good

good of mankind, that you will not publish the *Treatise* in question: Or, if this be already done, that you will forbid the further sale of it, and thereby remedy the mischief as much as possible.

But after all, I hope I am combating a man of straw; and that you have no such design in view, as I have been informed of; to be assured of which, from your own pen, will afford a real satisfaction to,

My dear Friend,

Your's most sincerely and affectionately,

RICHARD HILL.

Hawkstone, Feb. 2, 1780.

A

WORD

TO THE

READER.

IT is possible some persons may have the curiosity to examine *The Blessings of Polygamy*, who yet give themselves little or no trouble about *the blessings of eternity*. To such I beg leave to put a very interesting question, and yet, I must own, a most unfashionable, a most unpolite, and, in general, a most unwelcome question. It is this. Have you ever seriously thought of death? Nay, startle not, for it is by no means foreign to the purpose: So far from it, that

every

every word I have been writing, and every word you have been reading, has a view to this one queſtion only. Why have I been proving the abſolute unlawfulneſs of Polygamy? Not to gratify curioſity; not to ſettle a point of no importance; but becauſe I am fully purſuaded that the practice of it is highly offenſive to God, and dangerous to the ſouls of men. For the very ſame reaſon, therefore, that I would write a diſſuaſive from Polygamy, I would write a diſſuaſive from every other ſin; and for the ſame reaſon why I would wiſh to avoid every ſin, I would wiſh to meet death with confidence; and this certainly cannot be done, without I ſeriouſly and frequently bring the hour of death to view. Surely, then, this is ſufficient reaſon for reſuming the queſtion. Have you ever ſeriouſly thought of death? If you have not, I think you will hardly deny that you are wholly unfit to launch into eternity. If you have ſeriouſly thought on death, then remember that as *the ſting of death is ſin,* ſo *the ſtrength of ſin is the law*; 1 Cor. xv. 56. and that before this law

there

there is none righteous, no not one; forasmuch as *all have sinned, and come short of the glory of God*: So that every door of hope by man's own imperfect obedience, being absolutely shut up, there is no other way of recovering the Divine favor, but *through the redemption that is in Jesus Christ,* Rom. iii. 10. 19, 20, &c. &c.

You may try to stifle the convictions of your own mind, by the soothing opium of pleasure, or by hiding yourself in the wild thickets of infidelity, still conscience will at times find you out, and tell you, with an unwelcome voice, that though you are the creature of a day, you have nevertheless an immortal part within you, which can never never die, and that you must very soon appear before the aweful tribunal of an holy God, where all the actions of your life, and even the most secret thoughts of your heart, will be laid open before an assembled world.

LET me intreat you seriously to consider these things. Believe me, I should be sincerely

cerely grieved to leave no other impreſſion on your mind than a jingle of *Polygamy, Bigamy* and *Monogamy;* and therefore that the foregoing Addreſs may anſwer ſome ſalutary end, I hope you will not think I impoſe a hard taſk on you, in requeſting you to return to your chamber, and there *to commune with your own heart,* if it be but for one quarter of an hour; and with a pious ejaculation to *him who ſeeth in ſecret,* beg that you may know the real ſtate of your ſoul, if (like that of the rich preſumptuous fool in the goſpel) it ſhould *this night be required of you.*

ERRATA.

The little leiſure the author had for the correction of the preſs, will, he hopes, plead his excuſe for ſeveral inaccuracies that appear in the foregoing work. However, the two following ones the reader is particularly deſired to amend.

p. 67, inſtead of "who is ſo excluſively ſtiled by the apoſtle HER OWN PROPER HUSBAND," *r.* "WHOSE OWN PROPER HUSBAND he is ſo excluſively ſtiled by the apoſtle."

p. 147, inſtead of "women and children to too much, &c." *r.* "women and children too to much, &c."

www.ingramcontent.com/pod-product-compliance
Lightning Source LLC
Chambersburg PA
CBHW022115160426
43197CB00009B/1032